Marketing Strategy in Action

Alfred Tack

Gower

Published by
Gower Publishing Company Limited,
Gower House,
Croft Road,
Aldershot,
Hants GU11 3HR,
England

British Library Cataloguing in Publication Data
Tack, Alfred
Marketing Strategy in Action
1. Marketing
I. Title
658.8 HF5415

ISBN 0-566-02668-6

Typeset in Great Britain
by Graphic Studios (Southern) Ltd, Godalming, Surrey.
Printed and bound in Great Britain
by Billing and Sons Ltd, Worcester

Contents

1 From Advertising to Publishing

Mike Harley knew that it was make-your-mind-up time. Having sought advice and considered every aspect of the problem yet again, he could no longer delay a decision.

Leaning back in his chair, feet on the pinewood dining table, he once more studied the letter received four weeks earlier from solicitors Brown & Prewett, following the death of his uncle, Thomas Harley.

Uncle Thomas and Mike's father, Richard, had both been in the book trade since leaving school. Fifty years earlier the twin brothers had formed their own company, Harley Brothers Publishers Ltd. Over the years they built a reputation for publishing authors of repute and Harley became a name revered in the book trade. Richard had died aged seventy-five, and Thomas two years later.

Unfortunately the Harleys, after years of growth, had for too long lived on their past successes, unable to come to terms with the modern-day reading needs of frustrated housewives, permissive-society teenagers, and middle-aged males envious of the freedom of the teenagers.

Their latterday profitability was due to their back list of educational and scientific books – plus three best selling authors: the romantic novelist, Lilian Greystone, now aged seventy; the historical novelist, Hugo Parkins, seventy-two; and the humorist, S.J. Lincoln, a youthful sixty-eight.

The Harleys were held in such high esteem by literary

agents and authors that they were often the first to be offered blockbusters, the backstage stories of stage and screen, and pseudo-scientific star war epics. It was said of them that they should be in *The Guinness Book of Records* for refusing so many books which subsequently became bestsellers.

Mike Harley thought of his lovable father and eccentric uncle and their sadness when, having declined their offer to join the family business, he had become a star in the advertising firmament. Advertising – with its jingles, nudes, and the too-good-to-be-true mums and their children – was anathema to the brothers. Now forty-two, Mike had been in advertising since leaving university at the age of twenty-three. Moving from one company to another, he gained all-round experience before specialising in marketing, which included an ability to persuade top-flight advertisers to switch to his agency. Harley had, however, always stopped short of starting up his own agency. He was seriously contemplating this option five years earlier, when he had been approached by Masters & Grant, one of the United States' top three advertising agents. They offered him a package hard to refuse, including a free apartment in New York, more than double his current salary, an incentive scheme, very liberal expenses and other perks. He accepted their offer and became Vice-President, Marketing, with the promise that he would one day take over the presidential role.

On these terms he should have quickly acquired a small fortune. He did not do so. Soon after arriving in New York he met Debbie Clifton, the lovely but wild daughter of society hostess Alice and banker Brett Clifton.

Harley fell in love. Debbie thought she was in love and much against her parents' wishes they were married. Debbie spent even more than Mike could earn and he had to borrow to keep up the style of living to which she was accustomed. Two years later she divorced Mike on the grounds of neglect – untrue; that he was a workaholic – true; and a womaniser – untrue. Her clever counsel managed, by devious questioning, to inculcate in the judge's mind that Mike was having affair after affair while on location filming for TV advertisements, or attending conventions. The divorce was granted and Debbie took the house, furniture, cars and about half Mike's salary in alimony. He returned to living in the agency's New York apartment and it was there that he was contemplating his future.

The letter from solicitor Charles Prewett informed Mike that his uncle had left all the shares in Harley Brothers Publishers Ltd to his nephew, hoping that he would take command of the business and thus a Harley would remain in charge of the publishing house.

When Richard Harley had died two years after the death of his wife he had, by previous agreement, left his 50 per cent of the shares in the publishing company to bachelor brother Tom. The remainder of his estate had been divided between his three daughters in the knowledge that one day the shares of Harley Brothers Publishers Ltd would pass to his son, Michael.

That day had now arrived. In his letter Prewett pointed out that the CTT had been taken care of by insurances, that the company was solvent, but that profits had fallen considerably from the peak years. Prewett, a close family friend as well as the family solicitor, had suggested an early decision-making meeting.

The decision facing Mike was:

(a) to sell the business
(b) to allow the present managing director to run it, with Mike drawing dividends, or
(c) to give up his career in advertising and return to London, so as to control the company personally.

On first receiving Prewett's letter his instant reaction had been to sell the publishing company; but Thomas's will had stated that he hoped the business would remain in the family and that Michael would take charge. Although there was no sentiment in the advertising profession, and Mike was known as a tough, relentless negotiator, because of his love for his father and regard for Uncle Tom the plea, while not winning him over, did influence him not to make a quick decision to sell. He decided instead to investigate the publishing world.

Three times he flew to London, by Concorde, to discuss matters with Prewett and the Harley directors. Prewett was all for selling the business. The directors were for the status quo. What made him move from his initial stance was not Prewett, nor Uncle Tom's wishes – but Debbie.

He consulted his own New York lawyer, Miles Todruff, who pointed out that if he sold the business he would receive a reasonable capital sum, a part of which Debbie would soon be chasing – telling the judge that she couldn't manage on what Mike was allowing her. But if he left advertising and became involved in Harley Brothers Publishers Ltd, the salary he could draw would be about half what he was now earning.

The lawyer had smiled and said, "So you wouldn't be any worse off. Bardolf, your wife's lawyer, thought he was being very clever when he drew up the agreement. Because of your position with Masters & Grant the agreement stipulated that your wife was to receive an amount approximately half your salary at that time, with the proviso that she would also receive half of any subsequent increases in pay. I only agreed to that condition on your behalf if they agreed that there would be a total reduction if, for any reason, your pay should decrease. Bardolf advised Debbie to accept because, as he pointed out, your salary would inevitably go up and up, even if you moved to another agency. They could insure against your illness or accident but," the lawyer had laughed aloud, "Bardolf never considered you cutting your own salary in half."

Todruff had then continued, "As chief executive in your uncle's business, you don't need to be told of the financial options open to you – increased expenditure, for example. And Bardolf and Debbie would be the losers. My advice to you is to take over Harleys and perhaps sell out later when Debbie remarries, as she most surely will! You can leave me to deal with Bardolf when you're out of the country. I shall touch the judge's heart with my explanation that you have given up all for love of your late father and his brother."

Harley had not liked his lawyer's forthright views, but appreciated their effectiveness. He played back in his mind not only the conversation with the lawyer, but the biting insults hurled at him by Debbie, when she had found that life married to an advertising star did not mean continual partying in the world's more glamorous night spots, ski slopes and sunbathing scenes.

Then he thought again of the meeting he had had with George Beckworth of the great publishing house of Beckworth & Brooks. George, an old friend, had said, "If you want to get on the bandwaggon which will roll for a few years, take my advice and forget your bestsellers. Agents are killing the market by putting up books by key authors for auction. No such thing as loyalty any more – whoever pays the most gets the book – and more often than not we pay too much! The gilt's gone for us, and the weak don't even stand the chance of an opportunity to gain or lose money on books which might, or might not, be bestsellers. If I were starting up today I'd get on a bandwaggon that's on the road to success – and that's new style business books!"

Mike Harley deliberated for a few minutes more, then removing his feet from the table he began to compose his letter of resignation to Joel Masters, President of Masters & Grant.

2 Three Decisions

The waiting room was more like that of a Harley Street consultant than a legal authority. From bay windows to a wall-backed settee stretched a well-worn Turkish carpet surrounded by polished wood floors. In the centre of the room stood a mahogany table laden with magazines, mostly Sunday colour supplements. Prewett didn't like spending money unnecessarily. There were nine people waiting to see one or other of the partners.

At 10 a.m. precisely a young man entered the room and looked around inquiringly. Finally deciding that he had pinpointed his quarry, he invited Harley to join him, to be ushered subserviently towards his master's office.

All the clerks believed that it was a signal honour to work for Brown & Prewett and for a visitor to be seen personally by Charles Prewett was comparable with a call to Buckingham Palace or, at least, Downing Street. Such was the fame of the man – a fame which had turned a hard-working solicitor into a national figure.

That morning he was feeling particularly pleased with himself. He had won a considerable out-of-court payment for a cabinet minister accused in a newspaper article of having an affair with another cabinet minister's wife. The fact that the accusation was true made the victory all the more commendable in his eyes.

A timid knock – a voice called "Come" – the clerk opened the door and stood aside for Harley to enter the room. Prewett stood up to his full height and width of five feet six inches with a waistband of forty-six inches, but such was the personality of the man that few referred to him as "that short, fat, rather pompous solicitor", which would have been an apt description.

Skirting the desk he advanced a few paces to shake Harley's hand warmly.

"Welcome," he said – and again, "Welcome. Sit you down and tell me of your decision."

Harley sat down.

"Too early for a cigar?" inquired Prewett.

"Thank you, but I don't smoke."

"No, of course not! I remember now – how remiss of me!" And not waiting for an answer to his original request Prewett went on, "Michael, it's a splendid offer I've obtained for you. I've acted in your interests, although I do have a dual loyalty. Joseph Corbett is also a valued client of mine as well as being a very good friend. But as I explained to Joseph, your father and uncle were not only my oldest clients, going back to the days when I began my practice, but they, too, were dear friends. There could, therefore, be no balanced judgement on my part. I suggested to Joseph that he consulted another lawyer, but he wouldn't hear of it."

He paused, then added, "It means a great deal to me that in this era of general mistrust such entrepreneurs as Corbett trust me implicitly."

He paused again, and Harley smiled his acknowledgement that Prewett was a man to be trusted.

Prewett continued, "Corbett's offer through his publishing house, Brooke & Dean, is about 20 per cent higher than the objective I had set. But again, I personally carried out the negotiations, which went on for some days."

Harley thought, *and I shall get the bill for that sooner or later*! But he said, "I appreciate all that you have done, Mr Prewett." He could not bring himself to say Charles.

Prewett said, "Michael, it was a great pleasure. If the

position had been reversed your uncle would have acted with the same sense of duty. Now you have your say." But before Harley could begin Prewett was off again.

"You are probably not aware of the ramifications of the Talbot Development Corporation of which Corbett is chairman. They control companies as diverse as civil engineering, oil, property and car distribution. A success story and one man has built that giant corporation – Joseph Corbett." Tenting his fingers he continued, "His most recent acquisition is the publishing house of Brooke & Dean. He is taking a personal interest in that company and is looking for expansion from within and for further acquisitions."

Harley said, "How is it possible for someone with his diverse interests to be concerned with our relatively small publishing firm?"

"That is the greatness of the man. Even at top level he still interviews and selects his key personnel. He has been known to demand that all cheques over a certain figure on a particular day should be signed by him. But you know most entrepreneurs have their fingers on the pulse of their total affairs – a most remarkable feat of memory and time management! I want to emphasise that when you accept his offer he will tell you that you may remain with Harley Publishers if you wish and he will also be willing to offer you an appointment with the group's advisory division. There really isn't a great deal to talk about, is there Michael? The figures show that Harley Publishers have been fading fast and, Michael, forgive me for saying so, but with your limited, or rather, nil experience you could hardly be expected to turn things around. Sadly, these are the days of the big fellows with the cash to pay both accounts and their authors on due dates. Michael, I believe you are meeting Joseph Corbett at twelve noon?"

"Yes."

"He will possibly ask you to lunch in his directors'

dining room. He is a gourmet you know. His chef used to be at the Mavois restaurant in Paris. Now Michael, would you like to make any comments? You've read the report drawn up by my colleague, Scrutton – a very able fellow – which includes Corbett's offer. Let's get things moving quickly, shall we?"

Harley took a deep breath and said, "I'm refusing that offer, Mr Prewett. I'm determined to run Harley Brothers Publishers myself and turn it into a success." For the first time in many years Prewett was temporarily speechless, which was most unusual for him. Then he started to argue, but when he finally realised that Mike Harley was adamant he became exceedingly angry.

The Talbot Development Corporation building in Holborn mirrored the size of the corporation. Towering over the mini-skyscrapers nearby, its roof was almost large enough for a plane to land on, but the Corbett plane was kept at Gatwick. However, his helicopter frequently used the roof pad adjacent to the roof garden. He had fought long and hard and spent a considerable sum of money before permission for the landing pad had been granted.

Corbett's suite of offices on the top floor enabled picture-seeking newspaper or TV cameramen to show Corbett, from time to time, leaping from his helicopter before darting down the few steps to his office – always a sure publicity ruse. After a recent photograph, the newspaper caption had read 'High flyer lands safely again'.

Corbett seemed always to be bursting with health and energy, but the PROs and camera crews were not in the office to see the tycoon in his normal pill routine. For all his tough front, Joseph Corbett was a dedicated hypochondriac and pill swallower.

On the morning of Harley's arrival Corbett had made

his usual dash, waving aside his secretary in his hurry to get to the medicine chest. He was very concerned over the sharp, shooting pains in his stomach. Could they be an indication of something serious?

Joseph Corbett, fifty-two years old and a multi-millionaire, was temporarily unhappy and ill-tempered, and when in that condition he sacked a director, closed down a factory, bought up a company directed by someone he didn't like – or he went to see yet another physician.

He had allowed only fifteen minutes for the meeeting with Mike Harley. He had decided to buy up publishers, both in Britain and in the USA.

Corbett's office resembled a country lounge rather than an office: comfortable chairs, coffee tables, flowers, silver cups, paintings by Italian and Dutch masters.

The commissionaire on the ground floor had a list of the great man's daily appointments. Other callers were seen by his PA, or secretary, or turned away. Harley was immediately escorted to the Corbett personal lift which whisked him at high speed to the top floor. There he was greeted by Corbett's secretary – no model girl, this! Corbett's third wife had been a model and she knew what girls like models could do to men, especially middle-aged men. Corbett, after three years, was still very much in love with his wife and had engaged a secretary on her recommendation – a fifty-year old who was highly efficient.

There was no timid knock on the door from her. A tap and the handle turned at the same time.

The two men advanced towards each other. Harley saw a powerfully built man with a square jaw, a mop of black hair blow-waved to perfection and eyes so cold they looked like refrigerated marbles.

Corbett saw a well-built man with reddish-brown hair, alert eyes (Corbett always checked the eyes first) and a smile which, Corbett thought, augured well for the interview.

They shook hands; Corbett, indicating a comfortable chair for Harley, then sat down on a hardbacked chair facing his visitor. There were the usual pleasantries, then Corbett said, "I should like Reg Panton to join us. He's the managing director of Brooke & Dean, the publishers we took over about a year ago. You'll be working closely with him and I want him to be in the picture from the start of our co-operation. That's what I believe in, Michael – co-operation! Or is it Mike?"

"Mike."

"OK Mike, I'm Joe." Corbett picked up a radio messenger and instructed his secretary to send in Reginald Panton. Obviously awaiting the call, Panton appeared almost immediately.

After the introductions Corbett continued, "Well Mike, I assume you've spoken to Charles Prewett after you received my offer through him. I'll tell you this: I shall be the largest publisher of books in Europe. You can be sure of that! Harley Brothers are an old-fashioned company, but they have the kind of reputation I want and I'll soon modernise 'em. This is why, to save lengthy negotiations, I made you an unusually high offer. So Mike, all we have to do is shake hands. The lawyers will tie up the loose ends.

"You have to decide whether you want a clean break, or if you want to stay with us. I want you with us. You're the type of person we need. We want the kind of hard driver the USA advertising world so often spawns.

"Now you'll have to excuse me. I have another appointment, but we'll meet again for lunch at one-fifteen. In the meantime Reg will show you our legal department. When we meet again it will be to toast the future success of Corbett & Harley." He laughed for the first time, then stood up. So far as he was concerned the deal was settled.

Harley said, "Hasn't Charles Prewett telephoned you within the last hour?"

"Possibly, but I only returned to the office a few minutes before you arrived. Why do you ask?"

"Because I only came over here as an act of courtesy. I told Mr Prewett that I am not selling Harley's. I'm going to run the company myself."

As was Corbett's habit when confronted with the unexpected, he looked totally unperturbed. He smiled gently and looked benevolently at Harley, but he felt the twinge in his stomach which reminded him that he could be suffering from some serious ailment. "Mike," he said, "I appreciate your decision. I feel sure that you arrived at that decision for sentimental reasons – a Harley should remain in the business started by his father. But this is a cold hard world. There is no room for sentiment, although at heart I too – believe it or not – am a very sentimental person.

"There is no place today for the small book publisher. This is the era of the package deal: hardbacks, paperbacks, serial rights, maybe even the chance of a film. Think again Mike. Look, I'll ease your mind. You can stay as managing director of Harley's with a three-year contract. Agreed, Reg?"

Panton's well-worn face creased into a smile. His kindly brown eyes turned on Harley. He said, "I do, indeed! Yes, I think that would be right and proper."

Corbett said, "What do you say, Mike?"

"No thanks. I appreciate the offer but, no thanks."

The switch was remarkable. The smile left Corbett's face as his stomach twinge returned. His lips tightened. "Is that your final word, Mike?"

"Yes, Mr Corbett."

"No possibility of further negotiations?"

"No, I'm afraid not."

"Very well." Corbett stood up. He did not extend his hand, but gestured towards the door.

Harley said, "I'm sorry . . ."

"Don't apologise. You've nothing to apologise for, except wasting my time. Good morning."

Harley looked at Panton and hesitated about whether or not he should offer a handshake, but Panton, reading his mind, looked away.

Harley walked briskly out of Corbett's office, but not out of his life. The door had hardly closed behind him before Corbett said, "Nincompoop! He'd never have lasted the three years with me, anyway. You know my dictum, Reg – beat 'em, join 'em, take 'em over or smash 'em! We'll smash Harley's first and buy 'em later! And this is how we'll do it . . ."

Mike Harley sat in his late uncle's office staring at an enlarged photograph of the brothers Richard and Tom at the fiftieth anniversary dinner of the company. The partners' desk, sited centrally in the room, was surrounded by wall-to-wall shelving. On each shelf were heaped books, manuscripts and various packages, all identified by labels. Harley felt that to escape the cobweb era his first priority was to check on nothing, but have the shelves cleared, all packages disposed of and the office brightened.

He was not happy with himself. It was not that he was concerned over his decisions, or doubts that he could bring back some of the early glitter to Harley Brothers, but he had not acquitted himself well at the two earlier meetings.

The family owed much to Charles Prewett who, believing that he was acting in the best interests of his old friends, had advised that Harley Brothers should be sold. Mike felt that with hindsight he should have given some indication of his decision to Prewett much earlier. Yet that would not have been easy. He had only been in London six weeks, during which time he had used his marketing expertise to research the ramifications of publishing in general, and Harley Brothers in particular. Although on arrival in London his mind was 70 per cent made up that he would not sell, he wanted to retain the option of disposing of the business. It was only after arriving there that he had received Corbett's offer and had asked for time to consider the proposal. On reflection he felt that he should have kept Charles Prewett up to date with his thinking and not led him to believe that his advice would be taken.

He decided finally that he would write and apologise for his action in not showing the lawyer more consideration.

His mind switched then to the second meeting where he had immediately been confronted by Corbett who implied that his offer had been accepted. Harley felt sure that Prewett must have telephoned Corbett, but by the time he realised that Corbett was unaware of the earlier meeting, he had had no alternative but to listen to his monologue. It was during that monologue that he knew for sure that his decision not to sell and be employed by the tycoon was right.

He had met many Corbetts in his advertising days. Often they were dedicated parents, loving husbands, and extremely charitable men but, in business, ruthless and determined to win at all costs.

Looking at the photograph of the two old gentlemen he murmured, "How would both of you have tackled Corbett?"

He knew the answer. They would both have left the meeting saying, "We can't do business with that man. He is not our type!" Nevertheless, Corbett was the type to succeed.

He glanced at his watch and saw that it was 3.50 p.m., just ten minutes before the meeting with his co-directors. The thought of that meeting was yet another reason for his temporary despondency.

He had been hoping that by example and training he could instil some dynamism into the management team. Having met them several times he knew that was not possible, although he would still make the attempt. So much depended on his own efforts.

The right action would be for him to pay them off and engage executives whose management priorities were more in keeping with his own. He sighed. Surely, he thought, there must be a middle way between ruthlessness and management weakness. What could he do with them when they were all so certain that the book trade was 'different' and had to be treated differently?

When Thomas Harley had first been taken ill, some years earlier, he had appointed Kenneth Jason as managing director while he remained chairman. Jason had been in the book trade all his working life and had been with Harley's for twenty years. To him the job meant entertaining buyers and authors, attending conferences, travelling overseas to attend exhibitions and meet local agents, and giving final decisions as to which books should be published.

His pet phrase was, "In the book trade you have to maintain contacts". This meant more entertaining and was one of the reasons why Jason was on the way to becoming an alcoholic. But as Harley had been told so many times, Jason was a man much respected in the book trade.

The editorial director was Susan Clifford. She was extremely good at her job – one of the best in the country, Harley had been told. She had adored both Richard and Thomas and had now transferred her regard to Kenneth Jason. Because of this regard she never strongly disputed decisions she knew were wrong and that meant too many mistakes were being made. Harley still believed it possible that her outlook could be changed.

Clive Chapman, sales director, had once been the

London rep – Chapman called all his men in the field 'reps'. Harley was determined that they would stop being reps and become salesmen.

Chapman believed that if times were difficult it was due to incompetent booksellers or difficult buyers, but was certainly nothing to do with the reps. Constantly he emphasised to Harley that it would be a disaster to attempt to bring 'slick' advertising techniques into the book world.

At four o'clock the three directors entered the den – it had always been called 'the den'. At Harley's invitation they sat down in a row facing him. He wasted no time. "If we are to succeed changes have to be made – and no one ever wants to change anything. The fact is, we are slowly fading away. That fade must stop! Now, following our previous discussions, have you come up with any new ideas?"

He looked first at Jason, whose reddish broken-veined complexion told its own story; watery eyes, dark hair tinged with grey – a man with wife problems, children problems and, now, business problems.

Kenneth Jason said, "You've spoken about changes, Mike, but I have warned you that book people don't like changes. They like things taken slowly and steadily. I believe we are now on the right track and we shall win through. I was only talking the other day when I was lunching at the Savoy with Arnold Lyttleton – you know him, of course – about this very thing and he said . . ."

Harley held up his hand. "Sorry Kenneth, no anecdotes; let's keep to the facts. Have you thought of any action that we should take?"

"Yes. I was not due to go to the States until September but – " he took out his diary and studied it for a few moments, then continued, "I can go the first week in March, and see what I can pick up. On my return I can run a series of cocktail parties throughout the country, for book buyers and authors. We should get good PR mileage from that while, at the same time, cementing goodwill. I'd like you to attend each one of them if you can, so that I can introduce you. That's all at the moment."

Harley nodded, then turned to the editorial director. "And how about you, Susan?"

Susan Clifford, neatly dressed in a grey two-piece suit, her round face almost hidden by outsize spectacle frames, said: "We should try to capture a greater share of the romance market. We do, of course, have two best-sellers in Lilian Greystone and Hugo Parkins, but they won't be with us for ever! What we need is a constant stream of books which will perhaps never top the fiction lists, but will be steady sellers. We could do with perhaps two or three a month." She continued expounding her idea for some while, although not at all convincingly, Harley thought. Finally, turning to Clive Chapman she said, "You could sell them too, couldn't you Clive? We could have a new Romeo and Juliet type imprint."

Chapman, diminutive but podgy, said, "That market is already saturated, Susan, but if we could get some money for advertising or publicity we might be able to start a new imprint for romantic novels."

Harley interrupted. "I thought that advertising didn't sell books."

Before Chapman could reply, managing director Jason said, "I'll tell you our main problem, it's shortage of cash. Richard and Thomas were most conservative so far as money was concerned. They disliked, as they so often put it, being in the hands of the bankers. You can't generate enough cash flow to pay the advances that are demanded nowadays by authors whose books sell well with or without advertising.

"The larger publishers have all the advantages and with competition between publishers becoming extremely keen and authors and their agents becoming increasingly greedy, we shall have difficulty in adding any best-selling authors to our lists. I'm even afraid that our three mainstays may be enticed away.

"Can you find the cash to meet the demands for high advances?"

"Personally, no," answered Harley. "But I haven't yet got around to talking to our bankers, although I shall do so. But big advances always mean a gamble and at the moment we are in no position to take any gambles, and I doubt whether our future lies in first finding, and then competing for and holding, such authors. What's your opinion, Clive?"

Sitting upright in his chair, his feet barely touching the floor, Clive Chapman said, "We'll forget about romantic novels for the moment if you don't mind, Susan. But you are right in one respect: we can't sell if we haven't got the right books! Even our educational booklist is becoming out of date; there's a stream of bright young professors willing to write about every conceivable scientific and educational subject at cut rates. We should start looking around. It's all very well being loyal to our old-established authors, but many of them are now in their seventies and we have to think of the future. Please don't misunderstand me, Mike, we do publish really good books every month, otherwise we shouldn't make any profits. But there aren't enough to get excited about and salesmen have to get excited about their wares. My suggestion is that Susan takes on an additional editor to seek out good new books and we also engage two more reps. I should like an assistant as well, so that I could spend more time in the field. How about that for starters?"

Before Harley could reply there was a heated discussion. Jason and Susan justified their selection of books and blamed the sales department for not being good enough. Harley allowed the discussion to continue for a short time while the three protagonists were arguing. He thought: 'No one is ever wrong and few people can be convinced that they are wrong. Even when a managing director's company suffers heavy losses it is never through that managing director's wrong decisions. It is always due to other circumstances'.

Finally, Harley interrupted. "There isn't any point in continuing this 'right or wrong' discussion. Let me make some positive statements now and explain my plan for expansion."

Jason's face pictured his thoughts: 'What does this fellow know about publishing?'

Harley continued, "Kenneth, we'll have a chat about your suggestions." It wasn't right to slap down the managing director in front of his colleagues, but when they were alone he would spell out the fact that Jason was setting a bad example by spending too much on entertaining and showing lack of consideration for his lesser authors. This much he had learned from talking to the authors on the Harley Brothers' list.

He would tell Jason that he would have to prepare a cost-conscious itinerary for his US trip; many contacts in few days and no unnecessary entertaining. Also the PRO's last resort – cocktail parties – was out.

To Susan he said, "We should consider your idea of a romance imprint covering two or three books every month. Will you research, Susan, and then let Kenneth and me know whether you can obtain the books, what the costs will be, the price the market will stand for . . . OK?"

Susan Clifford, surprised that her idea had been found partly acceptable, blushed with pleasure.

To Clive Chapman Harley said, "Clive, you and I are going to have an in-depth discussion on marketing. We must find ways of helping booksellers to sell our books. We must overcome the despatch problem. But most of all, we must put all our salesmen through an intensive sales course. Oh, I know you can't sell books like detergents, but there is a middle way between hard selling and humbly requesting a buyer to look at your lists. And finally there will be a strong drive for cutting costs.

"Now, however, I am going to explain to you how we shall start an entirely different publishing venture and one which is going to be extremely successful.

"Some of the best sellers in the USA over the past two years have been business books. Their sales have been phenomenal. I am not referring to ordinary textbooks, but books that can be read and enjoyed, besides containing a mine of information.

"But the US have not yet capitalised on what has been happening. We shall!

"The problem with management textbooks is that they are usually so boring, in fact I doubt whether anyone ever reads them right through except perhaps the most avid students. Mostly they are written by academics or consultants who have not been active in management for many years. That doesn't mean that the books are bad – not at all! They are almost always very good books, but the reader finds difficulty in concentrating and so skips through them.

"We are going to publish books written by men and women who are active in management."

"It won't work," Jason said quietly. "Entrepreneurs, tycoons and managers generally can't write. I am referring, of course, to writing as an author."

"I agree," replied Harley, "but we are not going to ask them to write."

Jason looked puzzled. All the directors were listening intently. "What we are going to do," said Harley, "is invite active managers in many spheres of activity – finance, distribution, computers, general management, selling, retail management, hotel management, marketing – to participate in discussions which will lead to all-action, practical books. I shall have no trouble in finding the right men and women specialists and I'll invite them to meet for a week at a country hotel. They will be motivated, mainly, by shared royalties, ego building, and an opportunity to express their views to a larger public, as well as being able to tell associates and friends, 'Harleys, the well-known publishers, asked me . . .'

"Each session will be recorded, and you, Susan, will arrange for the recordings to be edited, and turned into a book. And that book will be a bestseller!

"It will be factual, anecdotal, but most of all, it will be practical. And the first book to be published by Harley Brothers will be *Marketing Strategy in Action*."

3 New Venture Management Books – Memorandum on Progress

Date: 15 March

To: K. Jason
S. Clifford
C. Chapman

From: M. Harley

OBJECTIVE

To enlist four outstanding and articulate marketing executives to take part in a recorded five-day seminar.

FINDING PARTICIPANTS

Contacts made during my years in advertising.
Classified advertisements in *Daily Telegraph* and *The Times*, small space advertisements in *Marketing* and *Marketing Week*.

RESULTS

Thirty-eight replies from advertisements, all contacted by telephone.
Fourteen interviewed.
Two chosen.

Two further executives selected from my previous contacts.

PLACE AND TIME

The seminar will be held at the Pellew Grange Hotel in the New Forest.
The four marketeers will arrive on Sunday 4 June.
The seminar will begin at 9 a.m. on 5 June and end with a farewell luncheon or dinner on Friday 9 June, at which I should like all of you to be present.
Further details will be sent to you later.

MEMBERS OF MARKETING SYNDICATE

Cathy James, marketing director, Caring Hygiene Services – a personal contact.
Mrs James has been with Caring for about ten years as a member of the sales team, later becoming sales manager. She is now on the main board.
Caring manufactures a wide range of hygiene equipment, including disposal units, soap dispensers, paper roller towels, hand dryers, air purifiers and air fresheners. The company employs two hundred sales staff and a similar number of service operators. Its markets include local authorities, shops, offices, factories, food establishments.
They sell direct, but not to private homes.

Colin Drake, marketing director, Foster Biscuits PLC – another of my contacts. He has always been in fast-moving consumer goods and was headhunted from Tamworth Smith about six years ago.
Fosters sells to wholesalers who cover small retail and restaurant outlets, but direct to retail multiples, superstores, hospitals and other large buyers.
It is an old-established but very dynamic organisation.

Bruce Hayes, marketing director, Atlantis Life. As a salesman he was highly successful and has been a supervisor, area manager, regional manager and sales manager for Atlantis, before being promoted to the board. His division employs about two thousand salesmen selling life assurance.

Ian Ashton, marketing director, Waltham & Duckworth Ltd. Ashton is a highly qualified engineer. Before taking charge of overall marketing he was the export sales manager.
Waltham & Duckworth manufactures a wide range of engineering products, including dust extractors, smoke dispersal units and industrial heating equipment.
The objective of its fifteen technical salesmen in this country is to have W & D products specified by architects, consulting engineers and main contractors.

You will agree that these directors cover a wide spectrum of marketing and I know each will contribute to a worthwhile book.

Please advise me if there are any specific areas you wish to discuss, to the benefit of the finished book.

4 The Marketing Objectives

Pellew Grange was one of the new breed of country hotels which received star awards from the tribe of gourmets who contributed to good food guides. Mostly they follow the same pattern – chintzy bedrooms, dining room and corridor walls covered with paintings, prints, graphics and usually against a flocked wallpaper background. A swimming pool and snooker room to help those attending seminars and conventions to while away the leisure hours.

Sunday evening when the selected marketeers first met had passed off well. Harley had insisted that marketing would not be discussed before the first session began on the next morning. They regaled each other with talk of holiday experiences, children's achievements, sport and their early days of struggle.

At 9 a.m. on the Monday they entered the meeting room. It contained furniture which could be arranged to suit the visitors' wishes and Harley had asked for the chairs to be set out in a semi-circle. Standing with his back to the bay window, he smiled his welcome, uttering the usual pleasantries – "Was your room OK?" "Did you sleep all right?" . . .

The first to sit down was Cathy James. At nineteen she had been a glamorous Miss Jersey and had lost little of that teenage glamour at thirty-five. Married at twenty-two, divorced at twenty-five, she had not remarried.

Quickly taking the seat on her left was Colin Drake of

Foster Biscuits. Thirty-seven, sandy hair curling onto his collar, a thin face offset by his square jaw, he still had the slim build of the outstanding sprinter he had been in his youth. Happily married, with three children, he still had an eye for a shapely figure.

But that also applied to Ian Ashton, who just beat Bruce Hayes to the seat on Cathy's right. Ian, some six feet tall, angular and wearing a badly-fitting suit, seemed to have a permanent expression of worry and concern. He was thirty-six, but looked ten years older, and it was said of him that he "worried his way to success".

Bruce Hayes looked the dynamic salesman he was. At forty-seven he was the oldest of those present. Over six feet tall, he carried little surplus fat. His hair was iron grey and his complexion pink. He had deep furrows running down each cheek which added to the dignity of his appearance. He was dedicated to life assurance and to his family – in that order, his wife maintained.

Glancing around to see that everyone was comfortable, Harley sat down facing his guests and opened the meeting.

"We shall have three sessions each day: mornings from nine until twelve noon, afternoons from two to four and from four-fifteen until six-fifteen. We'll finish on Friday at mid-day. These times are, of course, approximations. During this preliminary session we must decide on the style of the marketing book, our target readership, and the contents. First, let's have your views on style."

Without hesitation Cathy James said, "Not a standard textbook, surely . . ."

"Hold it," interrupted Harley, "I've forgotten to switch on the recorder."

Cathy said, "Do we need to record this preliminary session?"

"Why not?" Harley answered.

Cathy repeated her opening words, continuing, "I know your aim is to make it a highly readable book, that's why we're here. My plea is that we cut out the jargon.

"I was glancing through a marketing book before I left home and these are some of the phrases used: 'concentric diversification'; 'oliogopolistic market'; 'transactional efficiency' . . ."

"May I interrupt?" asked Ian Ashton.

Harley said, "Let's make the first rule: all interruptions welcome, but if anyone is in full spate and making a good marketing point, let 'em get on with it."

"You may interrupt me," said Cathy, flashing a smile at Ian which gave him great pleasure.

"Thank you Cathy," he said. "I'm part academic, I suppose, and in my line of country textbooks are essential reading!"

There was an immediate grunt of disagreement from Bruce Hayes, who said, "The textbooks you refer to, Ian, are mostly technical I should imagine. We are in marketing, not the servicing or the production of industrial equipment."

"Quite right," said Ashton affably, "but even textbooks could be made more readable. I was only interrupting to agree with Cathy, and to ask: Who is going to buy or borrow the book?"

Harley said, "I don't believe we should direct the book towards students. They much prefer to read the unpronounceables in the belief that they are involved in marketing's higher disciplines."

Colin Drake butted in: "Obviously, in the main, the book will appeal to all those in marketing and should be read by all managers. Every one of them must be made aware of marketing disciplines."

"A good point," agreed Harley. "But in the main it must be for marketing people generally. Any other views?"

"Yes," said Bruce Hayes, "the appeal should also be to managing directors who may, or may not, be marketing people. In smaller companies the managing director is usually also the marketing director."

"That's true," said Harley. "Anything else?"

Colin Drake said, "Shouldn't we begin by defining marketing? Most authors on the subject do."

"Oh no, not that again!" exclaimed Cathy James. "Isn't everyone bored to death with 'marketing determines customer needs and sets out to satisfy those needs'?

"I've been on several marketing courses and so much time is wasted initially on giving various definitions. Surely there can't be anyone in marketing today who doesn't know that the purpose of the total marketing mix is to satisfy customer needs. Don't let's debate it again!"

Drake said, "I agree with Cathy, especially as the majority, and I'm not being unkind, of managing directors only pay lip service to the formula anyway. Let's face the fact that it isn't lack of marketing definitions which is the problem, it's the managing directors' lack of willingness to ensure customer satisfaction. That willingness breaks down as soon as the production manager says, 'We can't do this, or that', or the distribution manager explains why a suggestion put forward by the sales division is impossible to carry out. Or more probably, it's when the financial director insists that it won't pay to invest in new machinery, no matter how much the customer will benefit.

"The problem with marketing is that too many managing directors are involved in finance, production, the takeover trail, fighting off bids . . . to be concerned about marketing. Sir John, our chairman and managing director, is different. He's right on the ball and that's why we're such a highly successful company."

Harley suggested, "How about some examples of customer needs not being met?"

"Sure!" said Hayes. "British banks are always advertising how they care for their customers and want to satisfy their needs. I wonder how much they thought about their customers when they decided to close on Saturday mornings, the only time in the week when many people can make use of their banking facilities. Did they carry out research? Did they ask for their customers' views? I doubt it! They weren't concerned with customer needs, they wanted to stop Saturday opening. Then Barclays returned to it and other banks followed suit, all claiming that they wanted to satisfy customer needs. Fine! But why hadn't they reached that conclusion in the first place? Lack of marketing appreciation, that's all!"

Harley glanced around the room and caught Cathy's eye. She smiled and said, "As you know, we offer a hygiene service and recently we were considering entering the disposable nappy market. Proctor & Gamble are, of course, the leaders in this field, especially in the USA. They are also a great marketing company, but even they slipped up by overlooking the standard marketing definition. Their disposable nappies are the number one worldwide brand – they introduced 'Pampers' in 1961. In the USA the market is now going on towards three billion dollars. Then Kimberley Clark entered the field. They produced a more expensive nappy, but to most mothers only the best is good enough for their children. Kimberley Clark entered the market nationally at the end of 1981 and now claim to control 23 per cent of the market, and the figure is rising.

"The point is that Proctor & Gamble then decided to spend heavily on rebuilding their many disposable nappy plants, the vice-chairman saying that it was their aim to produce the best nappies in the world. When they were dominating the market with their 'Pampers' shouldn't they, at that stage, have thought more about their customer needs for the future? They would then have pre-empted future competition."

"And did you decide to enter the field?" asked Harley.

"No, we thought it best to leave it to the giants. Maybe we shall enter at a later date, if we can produce a nappy that will satisfy customer needs even more than those currently being marketed."

Ian Ashton said, "I can give you an example. There used to be a very large British radiator industry. Well, there still is, but we don't command as much of the market as in the late sixties and early seventies. With the development of gas-fired boilers and pressed steel radiators there was a boom. The demand could not be met and the boom went on until the depression. Then foreign competitors entered the market with cheaper radiators, their manufacturers often backed by government subsidies. They took 30 per cent of the market from us.

"It's probably still difficult to compete on price, but the radiator people, when the boom was at its height, should have been able to forecast customer needs for radiators which could blend into elegant furnishing schemes and exotic bathrooms."

Harley was pleased with the way the directors were participating and he knew that Colin Drake would have a contribution to make. He looked inquiringly at him.

Drake said, "Surely an excellent example is the Swiss watch industry. They had the market to themselves for years, but did their marketing people ask the question: 'Are we satisfying future customer needs?'

"It wasn't until the Swiss market had practically collapsed that they finally decided to enter the field of electronic watches which was, and still is, dominated by the Japanese and Hong Kong manufacturers. Eventually a Swiss consortium produced 'Swatch', a quartz watch. Other manufacturers dusted themselves down, got rid of the cobwebs and entered the more expensive electronic watch market; and from something like 3 per cent of the market ten years ago, they are now heading for 30 per cent. But how was it that a country with practically a monopoly of watchmaking in the fifties was so badly shaken by competitors?

"Simply, they didn't attempt to satisfy customer needs when those needs changed. They are winning some of the markets back now, but it was a traumatic experience."

"What must be emphasised throughout the book," said Harley, "is that to satisfy customer needs there must be total commitment by the chief executive."

"May I come in again?" asked Hayes. "In life assurance there has to be total commitment on our part to satisfying client needs. As you know, we sell direct and sometimes we come in for a lot of stick. But the majority of companies do take great care to see that their clients' needs are fulfilled. Usually, however, the client doesn't know his needs.

"We, and this applies to many industrial companies as well, sometimes have to create the need and then turn it into a customer want. Therefore, marketing often means establishing a need of which the customer is unaware.

"A good example was given in a recent letter to the *Financial Times*. It is from the Controller, Trustee Savings Bank, Group Central Executive, R.J. Williams. The letter is headed 'Marketing Myopia'. I'll read it to you.

> Sir, – Christopher Lorenz (April 1) is quite right to highlight the lack of commitment to marketing principles outside the packaged goods sector.
> A major cause has been the error of assuming that the techniques that have been successful in marketing are the only ones. You don't sell excavators or, for that matter, house mortgages, by giving away plastic roses. The underlying marketing principles must apply, but the means of implementing them will differ radically between markets.
> In the case of financial services, for example, this process is still in the evolutionary stage, but is proceeding rapidly. Three apparent contradictions seem to have muddied the water: the customer creation/satisfaction process is critical, but personal

customers are often both ignorant and apathetic about financial products; the financial service revolution is broadening the scope of service providers, but, in practice, success still depends on identifying particular market niches and directing fire power accurately; and competitive response time to the introduction of a new financial product is very short, but the customer relationship that results may last a lifetime.

Many companies have either not faced up to the 'cultural revolution, and possibly an organisational one as well' that is involved, or have been repulsed by the magnitude of the task. Market research has not yet developed the techniques to be totally effective and credible in this market place.

Nevertheless Levitt's basic concept is still valid, and the companies that succeed in the next ten years will be those that build effective customer-oriented organisations with efficient customer-creating and customer-satisfying mechanisms."

"An excellent letter," said Harley. "Only a few years ago, to have suggested that marketing applied to financial services would have been ridiculed."

Harley waited for any further comments, then said, "Let us consider the contents of the book. Which marketing subjects do we include? Suggestions please!"

"There should be a chapter, possibly the first, on marketing objectives," said Colin Drake.

Ashton interrupted immediately. "Surely the objectives of marketing are the same as the objectives of the whole company, to maximise profits while maintaining customer goodwill?"

"That's true," answered Drake, "but there are other objectives; for example, whether to hold on to what we have, or to extend what we have, or diversify. Another objective could be to increase our share of the market while still working within certain economic restraints."

Harley agreed. "You're both right, of course, but I'm sure you will also agree with Ian that it is preferable to stress such objectives throughout the book, rather than in specific chapters."

Drake nodded his agreement.

Cathy James said, "I suppose the same applies to tackling competitors."

Harley agreed.

"Are we including finance as it applies to marketing?" Hayes asked.

"Yes," answered Harley, "but not in depth."

Cathy added, "Our company succeeded by good marketing, but more especially because of one of its facets – salesmanship. We employ two hundred saleswomen and they do a brilliant job. Shall we include a chapter on salesmanship? Selling can rarely succeed without good marketing, but good marketing will, sometimes, fail completely through lack of effective selling."

Harley asked for general views and then said, "Cathy, as you employ mostly saleswomen, whereas our other friends here employ mostly salesmen, we have to decide if we are going to refer to salespersons or sales people."

Cathy interrupted, "Our girls are sometimes referred to as salesmen. Most inquiries refer to salesmen anyway, so I think you should use 'salesmen' as a generic term to cover salesmen and saleswomen. Isn't that nice of me!"

Harley thanked her and went on, "It seems that we can't really tackle salesmanship in depth, it is too broad a subject. But why do salesmen achieve success and why do they fail? Any ideas on that?"

Although several suggestions were put forward, it was generally agreed that the main reason for the failure of salesmen was poor initial training and lack of motivation. It was decided to include a chapter on training and motivating a sales force, and one on telephone selling, since it was such an important part of the marketing activity for many companies. Further discussions resulted in a list of chapter headings which could be revised as the sessions progressed.

They stopped for coffee. After the break Harley asked, "Are there any other comments?"

"Yes," said Hayes. "In spite of what we have said about marketing objectives, we should have a total objective so far as the book is concerned. We are all involved in the book and we want to be proud of the finished product.

"The objective I always strive for in my sales bulletins is: *Inform, teach, and inspire*."

"Very well put," said Harley. "I'm sure we're all agreed on that!"

"That's great!" applauded Cathy.

"Bruce, you've got yourself a fan," Harley said, amidst laughter.

He paused, then continued, "Marketing is a state of mind as much as anything else. It is everyone's responsibility to ensure that the right goods arrive on time to the satisfaction of the customers. When a company is totally involved in marketing, that company can beat competition, fight depressions and succeed in spite of government restrictions. No marketing sector can succeed in isolation. We must preach the total concept."

There were further discussions until mid-day when the first session ended.

Harley felt that a good start had been made. In his bedroom later he was heading towards the bathroom when he noticed a message on the dressing table. He reached for the slip of paper and read: 'Please telephone Miss Clifford, urgently.' Picking up the telephone he dialled the receptionist and gave her the number of his London office. Soon he was talking to Susan Clifford.

"What's the problem, Susan?"

"It's the Browser Bookshops."

"What's the matter with them?"

"You know they're very big buyers. They have over forty shops devoted solely to selling books."

"So?"

"Our London rep – sorry, salesman – called on the central buying office this morning and came out with an order about a tenth the usual size."

"What was the reason?"

"None was given. The buyer said economies were being made, but that didn't make sense."

Harley thought for a moment, then asked, "Where's Clive? He's our sales director, why doesn't he contact them?"

"He's in Scotland. I did telephone him, but he told me to ring you. He's on his way back and will contact them tomorrow morning. Our rep was certain there's something wrong, because the other reps were getting their usual quota of orders."

"Who owns Browsers'?"

"An American company."

"Find out its name and ring me back. Leave a message for me if I'm involved in a session."

A few minutes later, a slightly perturbed Harley joined the others for pre-lunch drinks.

5 Research: its Principles and Scope

As he hoped that dinner would be a gourmet feast, Harley had decided on a snack in the coffee lounge for lunch. He nibbled a snippet of Cheddar cheese and a few dry biscuits, then left the hotel and made his way to the garden path leading to the wilderness of trees and bushes known locally as 'the forest' – a place for ambling and thinking. Skirting the gnarled roots of an old elm tree he heard, "Hi!" He turned and saw Cathy James.

Ninety-nine men out of a hundred, on seeing such a figure, would have felt their red corpuscles chasing each other in excitement. Harley was the hundredth. At that moment he did not want company – and especially not Cathy, whom he knew so well. He returned a desultory "Hi" and waited for her to join him.

"Mike, what's the trouble?"

"What do you mean, trouble?"

"Darling, we lived together for over six months before you went off to New York and found yourself a man-eating bride. Remember?"

"You don't want to go through all that again, surely! And anyway, you wouldn't come with me."

"Because you didn't want to get married, not to me anyway. And you had a job there. I hadn't."

Harley softened. "Let's forget the past, Cathy. I made a helluva mistake, I should have married you."

"I might have said no."

"Would you?"

"I can't remember, it's too long ago. But after those six months together I know all your moods. I watched you trying to make conversation over lunch, it was painful. You of all people, who are almost a compulsive talker. What's wrong? Are you worried that you've made a mistake about the book? I thought everything had gone splendidly and you've chosen a brilliant marketing team. I'm sure it will be successful."

"No, the book will be a bestseller."

As they manoeuvred their way past trees and bracken he told her about Susan Clifford's bombshell. He also explained that until all of his plans got under way the profits were not high enough to withstand a serious setback.

Cathy listened carefully then said, "I can't understand why you're so worried. Obviously there's been a mistake."

"What kind of a mistake?"

"Possibly one of communication. Think of some alternatives. The book buyer may have been instructed to cut down on stocks temporarily."

"Then why did the competition apparently get their standard orders?"

"Oh Mike, you know salesmen as well as I do! They never tell each other the truth."

Harley shook his head. "I can't credit that theory. If the salesmen's orders had been cut they would all have been too concerned not to talk to each other about what was happening to the Browser Bookshop business."

Cathy thought for a moment and then said, "There is an alternative. An old axiom in selling is that if a face doesn't fit even a bargain won't be ordered.

"Maybe the book buyer has been upset by your salesman, or possibly he's a new buyer. You should get some more information before you jump to conclusions. Perhaps the salesman has problems."

"You have a point there. He's a bit elderly, but

judging from the figures he's the outstanding salesman of the company. He gets a bit irascible at times, but I can't imagine him upsetting a buyer.

"I know in advertising, many an appropriation has been switched because of antipathy between the advertising manager and a brand or project manager. I'll check on that this afternoon. Thanks, Cathy! Come on, let's get back." He linked his arm in hers and they chatted all the way back to the hotel.

Relaxed and in better spirits, they joined the others in the conference room. Mike read their thoughts as he and Cathy took their seats.

He began, "Let's start with some general viewpoints on information seeking – market research."

Drake said, "All of us in the fast moving consumer goods field are well versed in research. We eat, sleep and dream it! I think that entitles me to make an important point which was partly touched on this morning. Others may disagree with this, but I look upon research as only a support for decision making. It's no different from information acquired by any other means.

"Too many managers believe that research results must be the deciding factor in decision making, but there are many other factors to be taken into consideration. IBM, one of the world's greatest companies and outstanding in every aspect of marketing, temporarily pulled out of home computers – and that, after a huge investment. They must have researched thoroughly. Did they overlook what might happen if . . . ? It is that *if* that is so intangible and often waved aside because everyone is eager to go ahead, regardless.

"Another outstanding company is Heinz. They introduced the 'Take-5', an excellent range of instant hot foods, but they stopped marketing it after about two years. They blamed the introduction of microwave ovens, but microwaves had been on the market for many years and sales were growing. Could this be an example of a negative being brushed aside by researchers determined to find a positive?"

Harley said, "You seem to be making out a case for less research."

"My goodness no! In fact, more research is needed. We never move without research, but my case is that more consideration should be given to reaction research, which means trying to discover the future actions of users, competitors, newspaper critics . . . I'm sure that research indicated a demand for the Sinclair cycle-cum-car. Reaction research would, possibly, have proved otherwise."

He spoke with the authoritative manner of a person used to giving his opinions fearlessly.

Bruce Hayes said, "I agree with Colin entirely. I also believe that decision makers considering research results can be misled by the emotional involvement of the reseacher. In the same way that politicians can prove that an adverse survey is really in their favour, so an emotionally involved researcher will brush aside the negatives and highlight only the positives. If a managing director himself is involved with a project, you can bet that whatever the results, the scheme/idea/product/service will go ahead. And," looking at Harley with a smile he added, "have you ever known an advertising wizard agree with any form of research which tended to show that others disagreed with his brainchild?"

"You're right," Harley agreed, "except of course when I was doing the creative work!"

After the laughter had subsided Cathy said, "My plea is for more thought to be given to the research needs of the small- to medium-sized companies. We should emphasise that so much can be achieved from a company's own archives – salesmen's reports, customer files, service engineers' instructions – also government publications and trade magazines . . .

"Information on the market can be obtained by investigating what *has happened* in the market, what *is now happening* in the market, what people say *will happen*."

She paused and Harley said, "Thank you Cathy. So let us consider how the average company can make good use of research. I'm sure we are all agreed that while the research format and its objectives may vary, basics remain the same. And basics must be the starting point for the smaller company about to invest in research.

"Even top management mistakes occur by overlooking basic principles. Every champion in every type of sport, at some time or another has said, 'I've got to get back to basics!' so let's first discuss the basic principles of market research and then go on to the use of research organisations."

Colin Drake said, "I think we should state early in the book the difference between 'marketing' research and 'market' research. Many of our readers may not be quite clear that there is a difference.

"Marketing research, or a marketing survey, means a study of methods of marketing or selling; while market research, or a market survey, means studying the market generally – the consumers, be they housewives, teenagers, the elderly, in the lower or higher income brackets, buyers in industry or decision makers for governments or local authorities.

"Research covers such a wide area that I can only outline some of the principles so far as the consumer market is concerned. First we have to consider the potential market. It is no use planning future strategies, advertising, investments, unless we have some idea of the potential market. Only then can we consider our objectives. Any comments?"

Ian Ashton said, "You mention the consumer market,

but your opening remarks certainly apply also to capital equipment. Too often new products are developed or old products changed on one person's whim, or a general belief. We always assess the potential market both here and overseas and then take a critical look at the market share of our competitors and our own market share. I'm making this point, Colin, because you may be one of the many managers who consider that marketing potential applies only to consumer goods."

Drake said, "I'm sorry I didn't make my position clear. I am talking mostly about the consumer market, but that doesn't mean that the application is not the same in the services or the industrial markets."

Bruce Hayes said, "It isn't quite so important in insurance, because we often have to react very quickly to changing conditions which are unpredictable; the effects of new taxation, for example."

Drake added, "But even then you have to consider the potential market. Surely you direct your salesmen to the most likely market for the policies you want to sell – the people most likely to react to the insurance – or is it assurance?"

"It can be either. Roughly, assurance implies a policy with a terminal payment or pension, while insurance can result in premiums being paid for a period of time with no final return, or payment only against fire, burglary, loss etc. Have a fire and we pay up; don't have a fire but you still have to keep up your payments, with no rebate at the end of a given period."

"Thanks for that information," said Harley, "which has absolutely nothing to do with potential markets, but adds to our general knowledge." And turning to Drake he said, "Had you finished?"

"Not quite. Returning to assurance, surely, Bruce, you attack the market with the greatest potential? In your case it would be the higher economic and social grades of the population."

Hayes nodded. "You're quite right, but I shall have more to say about that later."

Drake continued. "New products often fail because potential has not been correctly defined. Many government publications, trade association publications and research surveys give a strong indication of the potential market for practically all products. There is *Regional Trends,* published by the Central Statistical Office, which provides such information as where most telephones are installed, or domestic appliances sold. No marketing man should be without it.

"There must also be regular research to discover how we are faring in the market. A company may consider it is doing well with turnover increased and profits increased, but if its market share has not improved as much as that of its competitors, it isn't doing so well. In the USA Coca Cola, for example, are still the leaders for cola recipe drinks, but last year their share of the market increased by 3.5 per cent while Pepsi's went up by 5 per cent. The same applies to the UK, where Pepsi increased their share by almost one-third. Coca Cola are still the leaders and are still highly successful, but not so successful as they should be because they have allowed Pepsi Cola to catch up with them."

Colin paused and waited for someone to make a remark. Nobody did, so he added, "Now let someone else take a turn."

He patted Cathy on the shoulder and she smiled and said, "Still on market potential, it's rather sad that so many people use their savings or redundancy pay to enter a market which is already adequately covered. They're nearly always too late to succeed. There's still a great boom in fast food restaurants, but I should imagine there isn't much potential left for newcomers.

"But Bill Jones is easily persuaded to use his redundancy money to open a sandwich bar or a hot potato stall. He doesn't stand a chance! He hasn't studied the potential and doesn't appreciate that the best sites in the High Streets have already been taken. He knows little about research or market potential. So Bill goes ahead, loses his money and blames everyone and everything except himself."

Bruce Hayes agreed. "It isn't only the Bills who lose their money. We have a division for investing in possible future successes. Many large and well-run companies will seek funds for expansion in a market already too well covered. It happened in computers, videos, cameras, employment bureaux . . .

"There is still an opportunity to succeed in almost every type of business, but only if someone has that proverbial better mousetrap – and even then, there could be failure without research and a marketing policy.

"Many an able businessman is so eager to plunge into a booming market that he will not listen to what research proves, the market is already overcrowded. He is motivated by the others who are said to have made millions. Our investment division now sets down very strict rules before loaning money. Before a product or service is launched, or a new market entered, there must be research to discover the potential of that market and the scope for future expansion. Whether the investment money is redundancy pay or borrowed millions doesn't really matter, the basic rules still apply."

Harley noticed the rapport building up between members of the team and also that they were not keeping to generally accepted facts of research, but were prepared to branch out into directions not usually covered.

Hayes continued. "My next point covers product design and user reactions. It isn't only for new products that customer reaction should be sought. There should be continual research into customer responses.

"A field greatly in need of research is packaging. Too many manufacturers have blind spots so far as their packaging is concerned. They ignore research in case what they believe to be perfect is found to be imperfect. The direction may read: 'Press side to open'. I wonder if the designers have ever asked their wives to press the sides of those boxes, to see how easy it is to get a thumbful of detergent or a broken finger nail.

"Milk cartons are even worse. The directions are: 'Pull up sides to make a spout'. Quite impossible! But perhaps this is a deliberate policy, because the waste of milk due to following these instructions must be enormous. Other containers need the strength of a weightlifter to push, tear or open. Then there are shirt packings – pin receptacles with every pin ready to draw blood.

"Would anyone else like to comment?"

Cathy added, "We make a hand dryer and are constantly carrying out surveys to discover customers' reactions. Since these surveys started we have improved the efficiency of the dryer by a good 30 per cent and all because of advice from our customers."

Hayes said, "But wouldn't a service engineer be able to give you that information?"

"Not necessarily. Engineers only deal with faults and are not much involved in design improvement. The customers would like improvements but they don't necessarily mention them unless their views have been sought."

Ashton said, "Your company is unusual. Most managers automatically fight any change. They rarely consider marketing requirements, only the ease of manufacture. But there is one point in their favour; it is possible to improve yourself into bankruptcy. Commonsense must be applied. All changes must relate to the market price obtainable as well as technical and production needs.

"It's surprising, too, how often research will help to create new ideas from customers' suggestions. A buyer, when questioned, might say, 'Why don't you do this, why don't you do that, why don't you change to, we find now that the demand is for . . .'

"Salesmen should be taught how to ask the right questions which might lead to customers' suggestions for changes."

Bruce Hayes interrupted, "I agree with Colin. I was speaking to the director of a Japanese car manufacturer. He told me that Western manufacturers were always complaining about being outsold, but they have only themselves to blame. He said our car producers don't research enough. They don't seek the advice of their customers or, if they do, they think the customers are wrong. They had discovered by research that the majority of their buyers were ordering extras such as air conditioning, cassette players and other gimmicks, so they decided to incorporate all of them into their cars. Naturally there was an extra cost, but their increased sales took care of that. Customers would tell their friends about the no-cost extras, even including a recorded voice telling the driver his lights were on when they shouldn't be, or a door was unlocked. They gave the customers what they wanted and Western manufacturers followed suit, but that was two years later." Hayes concluded, "It's intensive research that keeps the Japs ahead."

After a short discussion, Harley said, "I'll take my turn now. I want to make two points: distribution and timing. I could cite several cases of companies researching and getting their products right, only to be let down subsequently by distribution weaknesses. This could be caused by local depots being badly serviced for stocks, or wholesalers' requirements not correctly assessed, or poor warehousing. In direct selling, orders are taken, deliveries promised for ten to fourteen days; but deliveries are held up because the market has been misread. Poor research again, followed by customer dissatisfaction.

"Research will often show what is required of distribution. Distribution, to be effective, has to be costed correctly and the products channelled to the right outlets – outlets depending on the buying habits of customers or customers' customers. Research will also show if dealers have the ability, the qualifications and finance to ensure good distribution on their part. There must always be a research plan for distribution both before a product launch and subsequently, to check results.

"Another aspect of research is to ensure that the time of the launch is right. Companies will sometimes launch a product at the wrong time and even in the wrong place. Problems are overlooked, buying patterns ignored, peaks and troughs brushed aside. Because a date has been fixed for a launch, outside factors are not considered. This applies particularly to the smaller companies, who claim that they cannot afford to put off a launch.

"Timing is all important and research will often show the right or wrong time to launch a product or service. That concludes my piece on distribution and timing."

Drake said, "Mike, how about research into advertising?"

Harley replied, "I think it best if we discuss that subject when we have a session on advertising."

Drake nodded and Harley, turning to Cathy, said, "We'd like to hear your views on sales research."

Cathy looked pleased at being asked to talk about her favourite subject, salesmanship. Although she was marketing director and up to date with all the marketing disciplines, her success had been due to outstanding sales ability and the motivational control of her sales team.

She began. "Salesmen are easily motivated, but just as easily demotivated. One of the demotivators is a wrongly set quota.

"How are quotas arrived at? Maybe the sales manager

is told that he has to increase turnover by 15 per cent during the following year. He solves that problem by increasing every salesman's quota by 15 per cent. Alternatively, he might invite his salesmen to suggest their own quotas so as to average out the 15 per cent increase. This usually means that the weak salesman, building his own ego and attempting to win more respect from his sales manager, puts in for a greatly increased quota, an objective he cannot achieve. The leading salesman, however, will often condition the sales manager's mind by complaining of problems ahead and then suggesting a modest increase in his turnover, a target which he is sure to beat.

"The right way to set quotas is by research. Of course we must listen to the salesmen and their points of view should be considered. A decision should however be made only after the consideration of many factors, for example the economic situation in various areas. Where there is high unemployment it is not always possible to reach the objective set by management. Then the extent of special sales drives or advertising campaigns and sales promotions must be taken into consideration. Next sales figures are extrapolated from recent results, not six or twelve months before; and returning to the potential, the sales manager should want to know the potential demands for each area.

"I want to emphasise that the standard method of issuing block quotas is wrong. Quotas must be assessed for each salesman and for each area and they must always be fair. Only research can substantiate the fairness of a salesman's quota. And the quota should not be inviolate for twelve months. There must also be a continual analysis of sales and trends so that quotas may be changed if necessary, although never to the detriment of the salesman's earnings if the quota has been previously agreed."

After a moment's pause Cathy went on, "As the book is not really directed at students, am I being too basic?"

"No," replied Harley. "We all know what we should do, but we need reminding that sometimes we must return to fundamentals. I intend to keep referring to this factor throughout the sessions. Now are there any other points you want to make, Cathy, regarding the selling function and research?"

"Yes. I have touched on this before, but I must repeat it: there should be a sales analysis by geographical areas – by types of user; analysis of buying trends; analysis of unit profitability which may vary from product to product – salesmen so often concentrate on products with the lower profit margins; analysis of repeat orders; analysis of complaints . . . That is all a part of the function of sales management.

"But there is another analysis and that's one we have been stressing throughout this session, but I should like to highlight it. It is analysis of customer reactions.

"May I tell you a true story concerning the way it was tackled by one company? The company is Troughtons, the house builders. They had made a heavy investment in developing a large building site. House designs had been submitted and approved by a committee, but not by John Troughton himself. He wanted to know the public's views, but was told that there was little use asking the public what they wanted because the public never considered costs when making their suggestions.

"John Troughton differed. He gave instructions that a model house was to be built, complete with all kitchen equipment etc. Then he arranged for fifty possible buyers to be contacted, not with a view to selling them a house, but solely to get their opinions. There were free gifts and lunches for those taking part in the survey. There was no problem in finding volunteers.

"Each visitor filled in a questionnaire, giving likes and dislikes and suggesting possible changes. These were considered and many of the ideas adopted. The clients were invited to return after the changes had been made and again asked to give their views and also to set a price which they would consider fair for the purchase of the house.

"Because the house now accorded so much with their views they all overstated the price. When told of the price Troughtons were charging – a figure which was lower than their guesstimates – several of them said they would buy, and some decided to think about it.

"Of these two also subsequently became purchasers, but the selling function had not been the main objective of the exercise. It was research to get the product right so that salesmen could sell with conviction.

"And that," concluded Cathy, "is the kind of research which, unfortunately, is not carried out by many house builders, or manufacturers for that matter. Except for test marketing of food products, the average manufacturer never gives the customer – be he retailer, distributor, engineer or consultant – a chance to air his views prior to manufacture. But this action alone creates goodwill and brings in more business."

More experiences were exchanged and case studies quoted. Then Harley said, "Are there any more basics, Colin? We have rather gone away from your original concept of research."

"I don't think that matters," replied Drake. "The whole idea of the book is to interest people. We don't want to keep repeating the same old clichés.

"Let's return again to the needs of the smaller companies. The managing director or his sales manager needs to research, particularly when profits decline. The questions to be answered are: Why is the break-even too high? Or: Why are the sales falling? Why are low-margin sales increasing, while highly profitable lines are sliding?

Why is everyone blaming everyone else for poor service, or distribution inefficiencies?

"This is the first step towards establishing the truth, and truths will emerge from research.

"In the larger organisations, especially where there is tough management at the top, middle management is always covering up so that no one will learn of the mistakes. Alternatively, middle management will not make decisions in case these should be wrong. Research will establish the truth. The first priority is to identify the problem which will highlight the objective of the research. The scope of the research must be established, who will carry it out, who will be responsible for its satisfactory conclusion.

"Having set the scene for the operation, the next step is to determine whether the factors on which the research will depend are within the control of the organisation. Those factors that can be controlled are price, policy, design, advertising, engaging of staff, changing attitudes. But there are also factors outside the company's control: strikes, market changes, competition, legislation, changing buying power. There may be one or a combination of several of these factors.

"The next question is, can all the information be provided by internal records and research or is external assistance needed?

"As we have already established, in every company's files, computers, minutes of meetings, there is a mine of information. Although managers complain that they are continually faced with too much reading matter, this is usually not true. In fact, managers don't read nearly enough, not even business sections of newspapers. How many managers, for example, have read the Government's excellent publications on quality control?

"If the objective of the research cannot be met from inside information, there are two alternatives: to use sales staff for research, or hand over the task to a professional research group. The latter is expensive, but it will provide more accurate information and analysis.

"I think that completes my contribution for the moment. Now will someone else take over and give the advantages or disadvantages of research consultants."

"You're doing fine," said Harley. "And you have the practical experience of working with professionals."

Smiling his thanks, Colin Drake said, "You'll have to bear with me for some repetition, but this is what a professional researcher will do:

1. He will analyse the problem and set out clearly the objective to be achieved.
2. He will evaluate all the information the company provides.
3. He will determine the number of people – customers, buyers, consumers – involved in achieving the objective.
4. He will select a sample from these people to give him the widest coverage of the total universe which, as you know, is the research word for all people, although some of our readers may not know this.
5. He will prepare the questionnaire.
6. He will make a pilot survey, to test the adequacy of the questionnaire.
7. He will train, or retrain, field staff.
8. Qualified field staff will carry out the survey.
9. Answers given to the interviewers, or received from the questionnaires, will be analysed.
10. A report will be made."

He paused and asked Harley if he wanted the book to contain details of statistical sampling methods used by the professionals. Harley agreed that they should be included.

Drake continued. "In brief, they are:

(a) random samples, based on totally random selections from the target population; to allow for the resultant potential error, the random samples usually need to be larger than other kinds
(b) quota samples, designed to ensure that the sample includes a fair selection of the different types of buyer in the market
(c) customised samples, even more precisely designed, so that the final sample is as nearly exactly representative as possible of the actual buyer population in terms of age, wealth, education, types of industry, size of company etc.
(d) multi-stage samples, carried out regularly over a longer period of time so that the information is constantly being kept up to date and allowance is made for any changes in attitudes or preferences over time.

"Although these samples should be statistically correct, there are sources of errors of which the professionals will be aware. They are:

people saying what they think they *should* say rather than what they really feel
biased or distorted samples
inherent communication problems which exist in all human communication processes; for example, a different interpretation of words
questions or questionnaires being biased in the way they are phrased
varying degrees of conscientiousness or subjectivity in researchers or respondents
respondents with certain characteristics replying more readily than other types of people
poor timing of surveys."

When Drake stopped, Cathy asked, "How is the research agency selected?"

"Sometimes by recommendation from an advertising

agency," said Colin, "but if, for some reason, this advice is unobtainable, there is only one way of being reasonably sure of selecting the right agency.

"First, bear in mind that it need not be one of the largest groups. There are many enthusiastic skilled researchers who control small organisations, but they are very efficient.

"The list of research groups, large and small, can be obtained from the Association of Market Survey Organisations. Select three or four research companies from the list and let them make their proposals. Ask each of them to provide the names of six satisfied clients with whom they've worked during the previous twelve months. Going back years may not help; personnel change so quickly in the research world.

"Contact the clients by telephone or even by a personal call, but not by letter, and find out from them the strengths and weaknesses of the various research agencies. Be biased towards the researcher who has worked in a similar field to your own. The odds will then be in your favour that you have chosen the right research group.

"Remember, every research group has one or two satisfied clients but also, possibly, a number of dissatisfied ones. By insisting on six names you will be carrying out a good research test yourself and researching the researcher."

Drake paused, turned to Mike and added, "Are you sure you want to cover all the basics? Most marketing people, surely, are well aware of the research needs."

Harley said, "You're wrong, Colin. Top management is aware of the need for human relations in industry, but they often forget the basic rules. They know they must acquire facts before making decisions, but they rarely investigate to find out whether they are, indeed, facts or are just based on generalisations. They require constant reminders of the need for quality control. Many managers don't know the nitty gritty of research. You, Colin, are so close to the subject that you believe everyone else has a similar knowledge to your own. They haven't, so carry on."

"If you say so," said Colin, and continued, "Earlier, I mentioned the objectives of a research consultant, but I didn't emphasise that survey work is based on the assumption that a large sample of the total group of people will reflect the characteristics of the whole group. A sample of a thousand people will give a margin of error, at the worst, of plus or minus 4 per cent. That's near enough for the purpose of arriving at a decision, but sampling one thousand people is really a job for the experts. I'm afraid I didn't make that point clear, but their strength is the capacity to select an appropriate sample. The average manager couldn't be expected to achieve the same result and neither could he have the statistical and analytical ability to evaluate the survey's results."

Ian Ashton interrupted. "I don't go all the way with you there. The sales manager might not have the expertise to organise a sample of a thousand people, but that usually only applies to the consumer field anyway. A good sales manager is quite capable of defining a problem and stating his objectives: customer research, dealer research, research for new products, or special research for advertising and packaging.

"He can easily carry out a survey by using his own service engineers or salesmen. They will get good results from questionnaires and I am sure the margin of error again won't be more than 4 per cent either way, provided of course the staff he uses receives a certain amount of training. If properly motivated they will research enthusiastically and not as an added chore to their already overburdened labours.

"A sales manager can develop questionnaires. Maybe they will not be quite as professional as those of experts, but good enough to provide opinions of what is right or wrong with a product or service. I'm sure the book will persuade many sales and marketing managers to try out their own researching skills first, before spending money on the professionals. If there is a problem in statistically evaluating the results of their efforts, there are many independent statisticians willing, for a relatively small fee, to analyse home grown research."

Harley said, "Thanks, Ian – and thank you, Colin. You are both right. It depends on the size of the research and the ability of sales management to carry out its own investigations. Now I'll take a turn.

"In advertising, it is always research, research and yet more research to discover customer or consumer preferences. There are many different methods used and, to a certain extent, I'm only elaborating Colin's summary.

"First, personal interviewing. If the interviewers are well trained, and that is the crux of the matter, they will ask the right questions and get truthful answers. The truth is most likely to emerge when someone is questioned personally. Interviewers are taught how to use snap questions which, almost always, get snap truthful answers. The main disadvantage is that costs are high and research companies sometimes employ untrained students who are unable to get true responses.

"The next technique, telephone interviewing, is extremely popular and again training is most important. If the interviewer is not skilled or properly trained he can do more harm than good. Telephone interviewing is economical; the problem is contacting the right people. It is surprising how many top people will answer a telephone call, even when they are guarded by a secretary. A managing director who ignores questionnaires will often give telephone interviews to a researcher.

"Telephone interviewing is a winner, especially with

the smaller businessman, provided there is an understanding of the presentation needed for telephone interviewing.

"Now, for the disadvantages. Questions must be limited and short. Interviewers quickly become disillusioned or unhappy after a number of refusals. Being cut off three times running can be very disheartening. Respondents also can be very annoyed at being disturbed by a telephone interviewer.

"Postal questionnaires, however, are more generally used. A wide coverage is obtainable and there can be careful selection. These days it is possible to identify any economic section of the community, such as an age group, types of voters, or the way we spend our time outside business.

"All companies can mail questionnaires from their own resources and although many of them may be wasted, a sufficient number are answered. Also there is no bias as there may be against an interviewer or telephone caller.

"Anyone like to add anything to these brief comments, before the tea break?"

No one volunteered, so Drake said, "I should like to add three aspects of research which have not yet been covered. Is that OK?"

"Of course!" said Harley.

Drake continued. "We have not covered brand barometers. These can be obtained from research organisations and they give estimates of the consumption of brands by all those in the market.

"Then there is the audit of retail sales, used by merchandising salesmen and by research organisations. The returns from the audit can be evaluated to give a clear indication of brands which sell and those which are given priority on shelves, or those which are pushed into a corner if given space at all.

"New product testing is a means whereby consumer acceptance of the new idea is tested by sampling products in various packages, colours etc., or even changing the ingredients for evaluation by a sample of consumers.

"That's all, but I thought these points ought to be covered."

Ashton then added, "Some laboratories will carry out tests not only on manufacturers' own products and the claims made for them, but also on competitors' products, which can be very helpful."

At that point the tea trolley was wheeled in.

After the break Harley invited Ashton to give his views on industrial research.

The gangling Ashton decided to stand up to make his presentation. Cathy thought she would love to take him to a good tailor and transform the badly dressed engineer into a marketing prince. On consideration, however, she thought that perhaps it was his non-conformist charm and undoubted integrity which made him seem so likeable.

Ashton began. "There's all too little research in the industrial field and therefore reactions to competitors' new developments are slow. In the consumer field it doesn't take long to re-package, or re-style, or change a formula to meet a competitor's claim for a new toothpaste, bar of soap or deodorant. But in the industrial field it can take a year or more to tool up when attempting to overtake a competitor.

"Industrial buying is mainly controlled by large companies, government departments and local authorities. The industrial field mostly comprises manufacturers of component parts, supplied to the ultimate manufacturer for assembly. This applies to cars, electrical appliances, excavators, or cranes, but such suppliers rarely carry out any research or plan ahead to take the risks out of a possible trade recession or a switch by the buyer to another supplier.

"Manufacturers should continually update ever-changing buying patterns. Those who rely on their past successes have little future.

"The key question is: What new products might be needed in five years' time; what component parts will be required? However small a company, someone should be appointed to research continually to discover weaknesses or strengths in both competitors and customers.

"Because industry regards research as applying mainly to the consumer field, industrial research groups are not held in high esteem. That will change. When outside researchers are employed, the exercise is often very hush-hush. Why? Because top management believe that little is wrong with their organisations, or that there is no justification for change or customer complaints.

"Another weakness is that industrial management is so scared of leaks, so secretive, that they object to giving the professional researchers too much information.

"A researcher, like a public relations officer, can only operate efficiently on information he receives and knowing the problems to be solved. The first questions a researcher should ask are: What is the objective? What is the problem?

"Some believe that researchers are not involved in problem solving only in providing facts, but this is wrong. For example, if a design is wrong sales will fall. The problem therefore, when designing, is to discover buyer preferences.

"If you, Colin, test out a biscuit, it is because you have a problem – to catch up with a competitor or to be a step ahead of a competitor. Your researcher will solve that problem by discovering your customers' preferences which will, it is hoped, be to the detriment of your competitor.

"A researcher can give statistical evidence for or against a future strategy. He should also develop feed-back signals, so that information on price and export demand can be continually received and evaluated.

"In my opinion, the time will come when a researcher will be as acceptable on the board of directors as accountants, engineers and economists are today. Then the researcher will be directly involved in strategy and forward planning. He will be continually assessing objectives and providing information to help in decision making. His role will be based not solely on marketing, but also on finance and corporate planning."

He concluded, "I rest my case on the plea that industry is falling behind in the research field and every managing director should inaugurate change by developing a strong research policy."

Bruce Hayes congratulated Ashton warmly, and said, "I am directly concerned with marketing life assurance, but our group also covers the whole field of insurance and finance and, indirectly, house mortgaging. Market research is now essential. In the professional field accountants and solicitors may now woo the public, but first they have to discover the right way to woo. It's all a question of whether or not bankers, accountants and solicitors will take the advice of the researcher, so that they will recognise clients' needs.

"Because these professional people believe they can do no wrong, they will do little researching for a long time ahead. Many will say they don't understand our profession and, of course, they will be right if the researchers are not given all the information they need.

"And that concludes my evidence."

There then followed a discussion on general applications of marketing services.

Harley suggested a five-minute break. Hurrying from the room he made for the reception desk and asked if there were any messages for him. There were none. He didn't know whether to feel happy or unhappy as he returned to the conference room.

The group returned to their seats as Harley said, "Let's conclude this session with some more general views on research."

Cathy James began. "May I make a plea for us to emphasise in the book that we should research not only into the strengths and weaknesses of our competitors' products, but also those of their managing teams. I was reading only the other day how during the Second World War General Montgomery researched carefully and continually into General Rommel's background. Monty put it this way: 'I wanted to get into his mind.' Why? So that he would know how Rommel was likely to think and act and how he could circumvent him. If we knew more about our competitors' top managers we should be able to get a better idea of how they make their decisions and what actions they are likely to take against our interests."

"Sorry Cathy," interrupted Ashton, "but that does seem a little far-fetched."

Cathy flushed angrily, but controlled herself. She said, "We've done it with success. When our sales campaign hit a leading competitor hard we knew exactly how their chief would react. He'd cut prices and try to take some of our best people away from us. By the time they took these steps we had held meetings and told our staff what we thought the competition would do and how we were going to beat them.

"They cut their price. We engaged additional sales staff and covered the ground more adequately, so their strategy failed. And because it was seen to be failing, none of our best people left us.

"Knowledge of competitors is all important. No detail is too small – how their receptionists handle telephone calls, lack of drive when they receive inquiries from newspaper advertising, and the way they handle complaints. We can't rely too much on salesmen for information about competitors, although they do keep us up to date to some extent; but a good researcher can provide much more objective information than the salesmen. I hope you agree with me, Mike."

"In this case," said Harley, "the editor's decision is not final. Let's talk about it."

They all agreed, eventually, that every aspect of research could be a benefit when fighting off competition. Then Hayes asked, "What are the general views on research committees?"

Ashton answered. "I believe they only apply to larger companies. Committees are better for controlling quality than they are for research. I think one person should have the overall responsibility for research."

Drake agreed and said, "We've covered the most important aspects of market research. May I summarise, even if it means more repetition:

1. Research is essential before a price increase or decrease. Will the increase cut production? If so, will this affect the production run? If the price is decreased, will the results so increase sales that production will be unable to cope?
2. Objectives must be defined exactly. Too wide a research can mean failed research. Simple objectives could be: Is an advertising campaign having impact? Why is brand *X* outselling brand *Y*? In your case, Ian, it might be to test whether there is a demand for a slimmer unit, a thicker unit, a higher unit, or a lower unit. Keep it simple is good advice, especially for beginners.
3. If market research is not carried out efficiently and if someone is not put in control, it will fail. It isn't good enough to hand over to Charles because Charles is not too busy at the moment, or to John, because John was once on the sales side. It may well be that Charles or John are the right people, but research must be carried out to find if someone is capable of doing that job.

4. Generalisation is not research. The 'everyone knows' syndrome; 'the whole trade agrees'; 'I was talking to the buyer and she told me . . .' are all generalisations in daily use and have a strong effect on managers. They should be listened to carefully and evaluated; but only research will give the true answers.

"My final statement, therefore, is beware of half-hearted research. It will surely lead to wrong decision making."

"Thanks Colin, and to you also, Ian, Cathy, and Bruce. I believe we have recorded a worthwhile session. I'd like to make three more points, but before that I want to refer to a brilliant chief executive, to show you that even such a person can make mistakes by ignoring research findings.

"Lee Iacocca, President of Ford and then Chrysler – a marketing man to his fingertips – wrote in his autobiography:

> And so we built a lot of cars with air conditioning, automatic transmission, velour upholstery, and electric windows, which added a couple of thousand dollars to the price. We should have paid more attention to our research. We had advance information that customers would be more interested in the basic model . . . It was a costly mistake . . .

"That certainly proves our point!" said Ashton.

Harley went on, "Colin told us how essential it is for research before entering any new market. I have some experience in this direction.

"Enthusiasm for a new product is essential; faith in one's own abilities, a great asset. There is often no substitute for experience, but ninety-nine times out of a hundred these assets are no substitute for careful research before entering a new market. Also all companies should have a marketing information system to provide the data essential for decision makers to plan ahead or make changes.

"And finally, we'll finish as we started – research is only a support for decision making. It is not designed to innovate, although this can often happen. Good market research will aid executives to arrive at the right decisions based on facts, not guesswork."

The discussion ended with all of them agreeing that they should meet for pre-dinner drinks at seven o'clock.

Once more, Harley hurried to the reception desk, where he was told that Miss Clifford had telephoned. He almost ran to his bedroom and was soon talking to Susan. "What news?" he asked.

"I phoned a friend of mine, Wendy Sayers, she's an editor working for Schuman's in New York and I asked her to make some inquiries for me. Wendy has just rung back to tell me that Browser Books has 150 outlets in the USA and is the parent company controlling its European counterpart.

"Browser Books, she told me, is owned by Cleveland Properties – and one of its biggest shareholders is Joseph Corbett!"

6 A Discussion

Cocktail time and dinner became 'let your hair down' time. Harley knew why. In spite of everyone's great experience in marketing, and they were all used to addressing meetings, there had been a feeling of unease, if not nervousness, at the thought of the task ahead. Would friendships be formed, or would there be one-upmanship? Would it be a bore when someone monopolised most of the time with his, or her, experiences? Would the book be unworthy of their efforts? How would they react towards each other? Would there be continual sniping . . . ?

But from cocktail time onwards it was obvious that all fears and concerns had disappeared. They all knew that the opening day had been successful and that each one of them had played a part in that success.

Harley realised that the first day was a 'make or break' day and he was well pleased with his team of marketing authors. He felt more certain than ever that he had hit on an idea which could lead to a successful series of books. The evening became quite hilarious. Even Ian Ashton contributed a series of very funny export stories.

At ten o'clock Ashton and Hayes decided to play snooker; Drake felt the need for a brisk walk; and Harley said to Cathy, "I need someone to talk to."

"That's not very flattering!" she replied.

"You know what I mean."

"Of course I do. Let's go into the lounge." But there was no quiet spot left in that restful area.

"It'll have to be my bedroom or yours," said Harley.

"If I didn't know you better . . ."

In Harley's bedroom they sat facing each other. In spite of his concern he couldn't help noticing her long shapely legs.

"Tell me!" said Cathy.

Harley told her.

Cathy said, "Now we know. But why all the deviousness?"

"Firstly," Mike replied, "the Trade – an umbrella word for booksellers, publishers, and trade associations – don't take kindly to publishers owning their own bookshops. But the important point is that so many tycoons these days like to act from behind the scenes. They have Luxembourg companies and Bahamian companies where their names don't even appear on the roll of directors."

Cathy said, "I see. But what kind of person is this Joseph Corbett?"

"A typical tycoon – must win at all costs! The type who would use psychological warfare to beat his ten-year old son at draughts." Harley then explained in greater detail his meeting with Corbett, the initial misunderstanding and the switch from affability to stony-faced antagonism when Corbett learned that Harley Brothers was not for sale.

"For once you didn't get your homework right!" said Cathy.

"That's right."

"If you had, you would have known that his reaction to not winning would be to try to close down Harley Brothers and then buy them out for a song."

He nodded.

"Mike, you're not the man I used to know. You were the craftiest, toughest of them all and you also believed in winning at all costs, so don't blame Joe Corbett for that!

You fought rival agencies with every trick in the book. Now admit it!"

"Well, maybe. But advertising is not book selling. I thought that was a most sedate, gentlemanly kind of business."

"Oh Mike, you're not that naive!"

"You didn't know my father and uncle."

"But they let the business slide, didn't they? Their methods didn't work at all – honesty yes, softness no; toughness yes, weakness no."

"You're right, of course, Cathy. I misjudged the situation totally."

"You didn't research into people – a point I made during our session. Now what would you do if you were Joseph Corbett?"

"Instruct my bookshops to buy as little as possible from Harley Brothers."

"Right! And next?"

"Try to take away the best of their employees."

"And that," said Cathy, "will be Joseph Corbett's next step. And you have to pre-empt his actions."

"It's a predicament."

"Why?"

"On the one hand I'd like to get rid of most of them, as I think they would like to get rid of me. But I wouldn't want that to happen too quickly, it should be a gradual process. That's the predicament. If Kenneth Jason, the present managing director, went next year I'd be glad to see the back of him. But right now we can't sell books if we don't get hold of the right books and Jason does know where to find the authors and how to keep them.

"Clive Chapman, the sales manager, isn't worth tuppence, but he's probably well-known to many booksellers.

"Susan Clifford, the editor, I could do something with. I'd rather she remained, but if she went it wouldn't cripple the business.

"Then there's the sales force. I'd like to change at least three of them, but not all at once.

"I could go to London, increase salaries, offer contracts; or I could sweat it out and let events take over, but that's not me. Somehow I have to keep the staff for at least a year, or even six months might do, but a sudden walk-out would really catch me on the hop."

"You're right, Mike, you can't stop the book sessions now and Joe Corbett has only made his first move this week, which is nearly three months after your original meeting with him. It may be that he'll play it slowly to make you realise you can't win and be willing to negotiate before he takes more decisive steps. It's going to be a battle and somehow you've got to win or it's back to the USA for you, with your ex-wife chasing you."

Harley nodded and said, "You've changed too, Cathy."

"In what way?"

"You're tougher!"

"I am not, but I have learned a lot more about men in business and how to handle them."

Harley smiled for the first time and said, "Well, it's marvellous being together again, Cathy. I shall go into action pretty soon – I've taken some, already – and I shall win! But I would like someone to talk to all the time. May I see you when we return to London?" He leaned forward and kissed her gently on the forehead.

"That was sweet!" said Cathy, standing up. "But let's leave it at that. Yes, of course we can meet in London."

She left Harley deep in thought and he soon arrived at some definite decisions.

7 The Importance of a Good Strategy

Harley slept well. He knew exactly what to do to beat Corbett and safeguard the future of Harley Brothers.

At 9 a.m. the second day's session got under way with Cathy asking, "What's the difference between forward planning and strategy?"

"In my opinion," Harley said, "the first objective is to decide on strategy, which can be to diversify, manufacture overseas, change the selling concept, open a local office, introduce new products, sampling to decide where growth will come from . . .

"Once the strategy has been decided, forward planning is the means whereby the objective of the strategy will be reached. OK?"

"Yes," answered Cathy.

Harley continued. "In this session we have to make out a case for a marketing strategy, which will not only be acceptable to our readers but will give them guidelines for immediate action.

"Ian, will you give us a general viewpoint and then we can discuss individual aspects in detail."

"Certainly," said Ian, standing up to address the group. He began. "Before we consider future strategy we must decide what business we are in. I believe that growth with the least risk is created by concentrating on our own business area and it can be a wide area. The giant multinationals regularly buy up companies in totally different markets and regularly fall flat on their faces. For example, the Imperial group bought the US Howard Johnson motel and restaurant chain for about 280 million and sold it later for about 255 million.

"British and American Tobacco unwisely bought International Stores and were much relieved to sell a few years later.

"However, because they are giants, they can get away with such strategic mistakes, which would cripple the average company. With smaller companies, growth comes from expansion within and diversification into areas with a common background. The background is not concerned with the products being marketed, but the business we are in.

"Cathy knows that she is not in pest control, soap dispensers and hand dryers. She is in the hygiene business and can plan strategically for growth in any of the hygiene areas, which can be industrial or household. Bruce has told us that his business is not life assurance, but investment and loaning money to all those in need of finance. Finance is the growth area. I am sure that his company's board are considering strategically many areas within the financial spectrum, therefore they are not in insurance, or assurance, but in the finance business.

"My company already provides a wide range of industrial equipment. For example, our smoke removers are in the safety business because in a fire smoke causes more deaths than burns. We are also in the health business because we manufacture dust extractors. So we can expand in all areas of health and safety.

"So lesson number one is base your strategy on knowing exactly what business you are in.

"My next point is that some say it is a difficult time for forward planning, but times have always been difficult for those who only plan half-heartedly for the future. There have always been problems ahead – wars, revolutions, shortages, gluts, oil prices up or down, economic shambles – alternative strategies can be worked out to meet most contingencies.

"Most boards of directors do plan ahead, but my plea is that marketing strategy should be planned in a more sophisticated manner and taken into greater consideration by main boards. Strategy applies to all of those involved in growth, production, research and development, distribution and finance. There can be no growth strategy if there are no funds to invest in change. Resources must be husbanded, particularly in the smaller businesses.

"In nearly every rags-to-riches biography and autobiography telling of the success of great leaders, tycoons and entrepreneurs, it is emphasised that they watched the pennies in their earlier lives. While the whiz kids were thinking of Rolls Royce cars, yachts and apartments in Florida, the future leaders of industry were busy ploughing back money and building reserves.

"All too often, spend-as-you-earn businessmen fail to reach their potential because at some time they make a mistake and have no reserves to fall back on.

"Now, over to you, Colin. Fosters are a large company, always expanding. What is your strategy to beat off competition?"

Drake said, "One strategy to beat competition is to cut prices, but we have found that is only a short-term solution. Unlike the carpet, curtain or furniture trade, where cut-price selling seems to be continual judging by TV advertisements, our strategies are based on providing a wonderful range of products and giving good service – and that is rarely possible if we cut prices. We make special offers, as do our competitors, but if the strategy is for continual special offers, then that must not be the sole benefit. Too many marketing directors overlook the fact that a heap of benefits can usually outweigh a competitor's discount or tuppence-off offer. A combination of these advantages, which must include benefits, is the best strategy.

"Our strategy for forward planning takes into consideration population growth, what will be the birthrate in a few years' time, what will be the lifespan in ten years' time, what effect will a change of government have, how we should react when a competitor's strategy is prevailing.

"Our marketing strategy is to ensure that we are highly profitable at present, while peering into the future.

"There is also inspirational strategy – a new idea, a new development.

"It was surely an inspiration which decided the directors of G.D. Searle, the United States pharmaceutical giants, to change their strategy when marketing a newly developed sweetener, Aspartame. Saccharin had dominated the sugar alternative market for years, but Aspartame had the advantage of being much nearer to the taste of sugar than saccharin. Saccharin is produced by many companies and sold to suppliers of sweeteners. It is marketed under different trade names by drinks manufacturers, food manufacturers and those concerned with slimming.

"Searles decided to change their strategic approach and sell Aspartame under their own trade name of NutraSweet to protect them from competition. They are spending huge sums on television advertising and it's paying off. NutraSweet has already become a best-known name in sweeteners. And now for the punch line: The price of NutraSweet is sky-high compared to saccharin. As I mentioned earlier, if the benefits are right, the product is right and marketing strategy is right, then price is of secondary importance."

"An excellent example," said Harley. "Unfortunately too many marketing directors have only one answer to beat off competition, and that is to cut prices. Sometimes this has to be done, but it can only be a short-term policy, as Colin said.

"Now, our next contribution, please – another verbal proof story would keep the readers' interest."

Cathy said, "We changed our strategy about ten years ago which, in my opinion, has been the main factor in our success. At that time we were well established, supplying wholesalers and retailers with own label soaps, germicides, fly sprays, air fresheners etc. We had very good products but were on the slide, due to the heavy advertising and marketing strategy of the multinationals in the health care field. Then we developed an electrically controlled fly killer, an electrically controlled air freshener and a hand dryer which we sold to the larger stores and retailers of electrical products.

"Selling was difficult. Retailers would demand assurances about advertising campaigns before agreeing to purchase worthwhile stocks, or else they wanted to buy on sale or return.

"At that time I was an area manager and also top saleswoman as far as the overall figures were concerned, particularly sales of electrical products. Our then managing director, a brilliant but ageing executive, decided to take stronger action.

"He formed a strategic marketing committee comprising himself, the financial director and the works director and he invited me to join the committee as the sales director had just left the company.

"We discussed every conceivable strategy and I suggested we changed our marketing policy.

"I said that we should stop supplying wholesalers and retailers and sell direct to users – not householders, but offices, factories, restaurants, hospitals etc. I was invited to submit a report. This, roughly, is what I wrote:

Speciality selling is so tough that I doubt whether any of our present salesmen could survive. The reason is that speciality salesmen form few friendly relationships; many sales are 'once only'.

When selling to retailers and wholesalers, however difficult the times, the salesman will still build a connection and even if he doesn't always get orders he is usually treated in a friendly manner. But for a direct-selling salesman there are no such greetings. First, there is the problem of getting in to see the person who can make the decision, who usually doesn't want to see an unknown salesman.

He is generally well guarded by a receptionist and a secretary. In the smaller businesses, hairdressers for example, proprietors are always busy, restaurant owners either cooking or buying, retailers serving . . . A salesman has to be very persuasive and most likeable to win through.

Speciality selling means being able to accept perhaps fifteen 'noes' to one 'yes' – that's the tough part – and only the toughest survive.

In the larger direct selling companies the turnover of salesmen can be almost 100 per cent each year.

That means training salesmen on a monthly basis; if twenty are trained, perhaps only five will last for two or three months. Of these, two may last for a few years and one could become a star. And the stars are the backbone of the direct selling sales force.

Training is essential and it must be excellent if the cost of maintaining a sales force is not to be so high as to make the business unprofitable. The training must be in the classroom and in the field. The regional manager must show the trainee how to put the fundamentals learned in the classroom into practice. The costs are high, but there is no 30 or 40 per cent discount to retailers and the rewards justify the outlay.

Direct selling means living up to the marketing concepts of satisfying a customer's wants by first establishing his needs.

Sales are mostly rewarded by high commission and low salary, that is why there is an ever changing sales force. No selling, no eating! But eventually a strong sales team can be developed.

It's a great way of marketing because no specialised company need be afraid of any multinational or heavy advertising. Everything depends on person-to-person selling and there isn't the slightest reason why a multinational can engage and train better speciality salesmen than the smaller companies. It all depends on the efficiency of the marketing manager or training manager.

Success depends on dynamism at the top; on everyone in an organisation being sales-minded; good interviewing; good training; good letter-writing; good use of the telephone . . .

Give me the chance and I'll build you a team that will be successful.

"I was given that chance, and now, we are the leaders in the field."

She paused, as the audience applauded.

"Thank you," Cathy said. "I must have sounded a bit big-headed."

"So what!" said Harley. "It's the big-heads, full of brains, that succeed. But that's another good example of how a change in marketing strategy can be successful."

"May I just add two points," asked Cathy, "so that no one will be misled? Our success didn't happen suddenly. We set a time objective of three years; to switch more quickly could have been disastrous. We couldn't risk losing our retail trade within a shorter period so we went step by step or, rather, area by area. In fact we set ourselves a series of objectives and I would advise anyone considering a change of strategy to adopt the same procedure.

"I appointed someone responsible for the completion of each activity – advertising, engaging and selection of staff, and a computer programme to cover rentals and service. The controls were all set, with the main board controlling the total strategy.

"We also tried to identify future problems; contingency plans were formed. That, in conclusion, was our story of a strategic change."

Everyone congratulated Cathy except Bruce Hayes, who said, "You've stolen my story! I haven't made much of a contribution so far, but I was going to explain the strategy we adopted – very similar to yours, Cathy. At one time all our policies were sold through agents: banks, estate agents, insurance middlemen etc. We, too, switched to selling direct and now we employ over 2,000 salesmen and women.

"Our board changed strategy after asking some simple questions relevant to growth:

> How do we increase our market?
> Answer: Expand or develop new markets.
> How do we develop new markets?
> Answer: By introducing a stream of different or, perhaps, if we're honest, we'd say different-sounding policies.
> Problem: Our competitors would follow suit within days or weeks.
> How, then, to find new outlets?
> Answer: Change our selling plans.

"We did and we, too, succeeded. In my opinion too many companies have out-of-date selling systems. I'm not suggesting that direct selling can possibly apply to the vast majority of products and industrial equipment, but it would pay every company now and again to consider a change of marketing or selling strategy.

"When thinking about marketing strategy, first consider some alternatives. Should our strategy be to increase the sales by increasing the sales force and concentrating on those territories most profitable to the company? Should we enlarge the territories to give better sales force better opportunities? Or should we reduce territories so that there can be more concentration? Should we provide more supervision, or be economical and give less supervision? Would that economy pay?

"How can we make our training more effective?

"If our pay plan is wrong we need not bother about marketing strategy, because no strategy will work for long.

"I recommend this kind of strategic planning by considering alternatives to every sales manager."

Cathy said, "I'm sorry if I stole your thunder."

Hayes laughed. "I was only joking. I was as intrigued as all the others by the story of the success of your company and yourself. Congratulations again!"

Harley looked around, encouraging further case studies.

Drake said, "Own-label products is a growth area and has become so successful that even leaders like Heinz, Campbells, Crosse & Blackwells and ourselves have had to rethink our strategies. Changes should be considered at every board meeting then problem solving can be tackled earlier and the problems obviated.

"We should have asked ourselves what would be our future strategy if own-label products really took off. We didn't! We got on the bandwaggon and supplied own-label goods ourselves, which is self-defeating. 'If you can't beat 'em, join 'em' is a fair dictum, but not before a battle has commenced."

Harley asked, "What about the smaller companies? How do they cope? What should their strategy be, to sit back and do nothing or to take action? What do their managing directors do when faced with such a situation? How can they plan their strategies?"

Drake said, "The rules don't vary. First make sure you get your finances right and don't try to out-advertise the big spenders, it's impossible! Keep the quality high; don't start a price-cutting war which others will win. Try to win through by giving better service, by employing more skilled salesmen who will help the retailers and will be able to put their case before buying committees.

"The important thing is the selling effort for the smaller companies. In spite of shelf problems, a good salesman can still persuade a manager to find space for his products, even when the headquarters of the multiples tell their managers what to put and what not to put on the shelves. Managers can still make decisions for themselves. Also there are thousands of independent shops to be wooed. Unfortunately the smaller manufacturers spend too little time on strategic planning, living from day to day and always complaining of the difficulties of the times.

"But the efficient smaller manufacturer only needs a tiny share of a market to make good profits and that can be achieved by those who have a continually updated marketing strategy."

After a short discussion Ashton said, "I'd like to talk about industrial marketing as against Colin's consumer marketing. In industrial selling it is rare for one person to be totally responsible for purchasing. One person may have a final decision but he is usually rubber-stamping something already decided by others.

"Industrial marketing strategy is based on the fact that four, five or six people have to be convinced of the extra benefits to be obtained by accepting a decision in your favour. This is a serious problem: how to influence such people as the technologist, the egoist, the thin skinned, the obstinate. These types may all be cogs in an industrial wheel. The egoist has to be made to feel important; the salesman may upset the technologist by disagreeing with him on a technical point; the thin skinned will see an insult in every answer to the objections he raises, while the obstinate person will disagree with everyone who disagrees with him.

"My company strategy is for every sales engineer to attend courses on human relations. The old adage that orders regularly go to the salesman who is liked, still applies. When one of my sales force tells me that he lost out to a competitor and doesn't know why, I tell him that the buyer probably preferred the competitor's salesman.

"Obviously there are many other reasons why orders are lost, but I am referring to those cases where all things are equal and that happens quite regularly.

"Of course, this is all too simple a strategy for some marketing people, who believe that strategy only applies to great decisions: changes in the marketing plan, or the advertising plan, or the character of the retail store. By the way, why doesn't someone think about changes in the attitudes of the assistants in retail stores? Now that would be a good strategy! Or changes in product?

"They are wrong! The best strategy relates to people and motivating them to give of their best.

"Of course, major strategies are all important and perhaps I am overstating my case. What I am emphasising is that minor strategies are important too and those are the ones which are overlooked, those are the ones which lose business.

"First, my advice is to consider your buyers; learn about them, understand them and then work out a strategy to win them over.

"It is true that the present high-tech explosion has led

marketing managers to believe that every customer wants more and more advanced high technical components or products. Marketing men may believe that the future lies in their products working faster, or being smaller, or being operated by only one switch, or made of unbreakable materials. But although we live in a great technical age we must remember that some products need not necessarily be advanced to the customers' satisfaction by new technology. It all depends on *what the customer needs and wants*.

"My next point is totally marketing-oriented – nothing to do with technology. In the industrial field today there are hundreds of manufacturers making similar products and selling similar service at similar prices. What, then, should be the right strategy for those who offer the same products as competitors at about the same price?

"In these cases we should not rely on salesmanship alone. Here we see the difference between selling and marketing. The main preoccupation of the sales manager is turnover, we all know that it should be profitable. But deep down, every sales manager appreciates that he is being judged on turnover. It is others who decide the costs. The production costs, borrowing costs, overhead costs; these are aspects over which the average sales manager has little control and in fact he is often only partly involved in pricing. It is therefore difficult to judge him on profitability. Salesmen themselves often concentrate on selling the product or services that they like best or that they find easiest to sell, which may not be the most profitable ones.

"Marketing, however, is concerned with profits. That is why it plans ahead. The marketing manager originates and controls the systematic analyses to discover the profitable salesman, the profitable areas, the profitable and contribution pricing – marginal costings and profitable investments for the future."

Harley interrupted. "Don't get carried away, Ian.

Remember we're covering strategy, not selling versus marketing."

But Ashton replied, "I'm making a point which, I think, does apply to strategy. That when all things are equal we know that the orders will often go to the salesman who is most trusted and liked, but we must also appreciate that marketing in these circumstances has to evolve the right strategy."

"And what is the right strategy?" asked Harley.

"It can only be based on discovering extra benefits. The sale can be likened to a set of old-fashioned scales; all the benefits are heaped on one pan and the buyers' demands and requirements on the other. To obtain the order the benefits must tilt the scales in the favour of the salesman. Therefore, when all things are equal, even a featherweight benefit can tip over the scale, so marketing strategy must be aimed at discovering the featherweight benefits. The salesman will discover the others himself.

"It is up to the marketing manager to seek and find these featherweight benefits – perhaps in research and development, the managing director's archives or the accounts department.

"I'm sorry to be so wordy, but you did say that we don't have to keep to the standard strategic guidelines laid down by the business schools and academics and talk from personal knowledge."

"I agree," replied Harley. "And you have done extremely well. You've made a very good contribution and I promise you, it won't be edited out!"

Bruce Hayes said, "As we are covering strategy in its widest form I would like to ask a question. Why isn't more consideration given to a strategy for letter writing? If I receive a personal letter, no matter how busy I am, I will respond within twenty-four hours. That's my strategy to maintain goodwill. When I originate letters however I am lucky if I receive a reply within fourteen days.

"OK, if for some reason all typists have 'flu at the same time and all typewriters have broken down, there is still the telephone. A goodwill call should be made either to deal with the questions raised by the letter writer or explain why an immediate response by letter isn't possible.

"It may cause some surprise however to know that this situation is worse in the USA than in Britain. They often don't reply to a letter at all. I wrote to eight US companies suggesting a possible co-operation. Only two replied.

"We then decided to run a sales competition, the prize being a visit to Miami. I wrote to the director of tourism in Miami asking for his co-operation and suggesting that he might like to write to our sales force telling them of the entertainments and interesting features of Miami. I assured him there would be forty to fifty winners. He didn't reply.

"Marketing directors are sometimes so involved in what they believe to be the higher-level strategies that they fail to appreciate that marketing strategy involves everyone within an organisation. How many managing directors check occasionally the type of letters sent out by the service managers, transport managers, or even their sales managers? If they did they could well be dismayed, and then take action.

"I have an example with me. The letter I am going to read was published in *Marketing Week*. I have deleted the names in case, inadvertently, they crept into the book. That would be wrong.

> As a lay reader of your publication I am interested as a consumer in the views and varied opinions expressed by the professionals. However the attached copy of a letter received from *X* is an

indication that the old adage – you cannot get something for nothing – applies to sales promotion.

'Dear —, Thank you for your letter dated 4 April from which we are sorry to hear of your dissatisfaction with our salt and pepper mills currently on offer. We are also sorry that you had to wait quite some time for the delivery to you.

This delay was occasioned by the great popularity of the items. You questioned the quality of these mills. We can honestly state that yours is the very first letter that has complained of their overall quality and we have now mailed 80,000 of these so frankly we are rather surprised at your disapproval. After all they are free! The only way we can think of satisfying your comments is to enclose a £1 voucher which we trust you will accept with our compliments and our renewed apologies for having disappointed you. Yours sincerely' "

As Hayes put the cutting aside he said, "And that letter was written by a marketing executive who possibly sees nothing wrong with it. But does such a letter really retain a customer's goodwill?

"Admittedly the customer was a bit carping. But he thought he was in the right and that's all that matters. Why state in the letter that it was the only complaint out of 80,000 other mills distributed? That doesn't mean that there were no complaints, only that possibly many people hadn't bothered to write. What the writer is implying is 'You're the type who always complains'. Is that good human relations? But then if we return anything to anyone the answer is nearly always, 'Nobody else complained'. A cliché which should never be used or implied by a marketing executive.

"Let us take another extract from the letter. 'We are surprised'. What this really means is 'We are not so surprised as annoyed that you should have the temerity to write to us on this subject'.

"Next, the letter reads: 'After all they are free'. Does that mean that a promotion can offer any rubbish because it's free?

"Finally, the offer of a £1 voucher is almost insulting.

"And if, in fact, that was the only letter received, then there is no excuse for not telephoning to apologise for the delivery problem and offering to send another unit.

"The objective of writing letters to those who complain is to win them over. Don't you agree?" They all agreed.

"Then let's do something about it! If a marketing director doesn't get worked up about his likes and dislikes, his drive for perfection, his hatred for all forms of inefficiency, then he should change his job."

Everyone applauded. Hayes said simply, "Thank you. I deserved that."

There was laughter as Harley said, "OK. So the need for a letter-writing strategy goes in the book."

Cathy said, "I'd like to ask a question. Does a change in strategy alter people's opinions of a company? I was thinking of Woolworths. To many of us Woolworths used to mean low prices, good value and not so good service. Their strategy evidently didn't succeed too well. There was a sell-out, a change of management and the new strategy was apparently to close down some stores which did not pay, buy into affiliated businesses and redesign the remaining stores. Also to create shops within shops. The new management also instigated a complete change in design of the stores.

"My question is, will people still think of that old Woolworths? The take-it-or-leave-it attitude of some of their assistants? Will customers flood back to Woolworths because of these cosmetic changes? Will their perceptiveness of the store alter? I don't know.

Simply put it is this: it's people who make or break a business. Would the best strategy have been to retrain the assistants, or the shop supervisors to assist the assistants, to do more for the customers?

"Marks and Spencer always offer good value and they give the extra – polite and helpful assistants.

"Would the right strategy have been to change the name and to train the staff more efficiently? Shop assistants should be made to believe that the customer, after their families, is the most important person in their lives. Why? Because the customer pays their wages. If good value was all that we were seeking we would all be buying from discount stores and markets."

Harley said, "We are not privy to Woolworths' management thinking, so we can only generalise from our point of view as marketeers and possible customers, but it's a good point you have raised Cathy. Can a change of strategy work when the name remains the same and most aspects of the business remain the same?"

A heated debate followed. No one disagreed with the strategy of training people to give better service, but there was disagreement about the changing of a household name.

Harley then invited some other strategic viewpoints.

Bruce Hayes said, "Sometimes it is necessary to change a strategy quickly. For example, my younger brother is in the pharmaceutical world – he is a salesman calling on doctors. His company, like others, was hit badly when the Government banned 1,700 branded drugs from the National Health Service and raised the price of prescriptions by 25 per cent. A fair percentage of a £1½ billion turnover was at risk. The company had to decide what strategy to adopt.

"The first reaction of the pharmaceutical companies was to fight back by advertising and lobbying. Doctors wrote to *The Times*. The letters usually began, 'Dear Sir, I am amazed at the Government's attitude . . .'

"This strategy succeeded to some extent because a few of the banned drugs were returned to the NHS list. The leading companies then decided to attack over-the-counter markets and co-operated with the National Pharmaceutical Association in an advertising campaign based on the importance of the chemist.

"The ads ran 'Ask your pharmacist. He knows best'. They then produced smaller packages of expensive drugs to appeal to those who couldn't afford the higher price of the large packs. The next strategy was to spend heavily on advertising brand names: cough relievers, headache easers, nerve calmers. They were aiming to persuade the public no longer to queue up at the doctor's waiting room for a household prescription, but to visit a knowledgeable chemist.

"There followed a big drive by the sales forces. Sometimes special divisions were set up to call on chemists and persuade them to stock the no longer listed drugs.

"Although it will take time for the pharmaceutical companies to make up for the losses and some will fail the larger groups will win through and the efficient smaller companies, by better marketing.

"All multinationals and large companies are not ponderous elephants when it comes to changing strategy. Some organisations may take six months or more to arrive at a decision to change, but the efficiently led companies do so very quickly. But because there are quite a number of ponderous elephants still about the good little 'uns will so often beat some of the big 'uns.

"Strategy must be constantly reviewed and changes made within hours, if necessary, rather than days. In fact making such a sudden switch in strategy usually implies that the managing director is a cracking good leader."

Suddenly, they all wanted to contribute a case study. Harley smiled as Cathy put up her hand like a schoolgirl, trying to attract her teacher's attention. "OK Cathy, but before you begin, I want to make a point.

"Each case study must offer a definite lesson which can be applied by marketing managers, whether working for a large company or a small one. Does that change your story, Cathy?"

"Not at all! I want to emphasise that when the going gets tough, too many managing directors go down market. That's been mentioned before. I want to highlight a case.

"My example is Barratt Development, the housebuilders. Barratt achieved great success in building and selling houses to first-time buyers, but they decided to change their strategy. They are now also building houses with prices near the £½ million mark, although the majority are not in such a high bracket. Possibly research showed that those in employment were doing better than ever and that there were now many successful entrepreneurs of small businesses about. Whatever the reason, Barratt switched from a successful strategy to an even more successful one.

"Of course they still do well with first-time buyers, but their up-market strategy proved that they were not stuck in a rut, even a paying rut! So remember, look up-market first when tackling marketing problems."

Bruce Hayes then said, "I should like to highlight a different aspect of strategy. The importance of innovation and a good trademark.

"With the arrival of synthetics, wool was kicked almost out of the market. It was drip dry everything and the future looked bleak for wool. Then the certification 'Woolmark' was introduced. A brilliant idea from Sir William Vines. Woolmark immediately became associated with quality. In spite of the prediction that wool would almost disappear from the market within a few years, wool not only survived but became a paramount market force.

"The trademark was licensed under very strict rules and licensees all over the world, including China, are now monitored regularly. Wool is back in fashion and it's due to one idea plus a brilliant trademark symbol.

"The lesson is, never give up trying and never say it's impossible or can't be done. A new idea can change a strategy and lead to greater success."

Ashton said, "I wondered why I am feeling so hot, I thought my vest was nylon, but it must be wool."

Cathy, pretending to look shocked, said, "Don't tell me you wear a vest!"

Ashton answered, "I'm afraid so. It's my wife's strategy for keeping all the girls away." There were some ribald remarks, then Ashton said, "Here's a poser for you. Can any of you tell me what the Lanchester strategy is?"

No one replied so Harley said: "Ian, we don't want academic theories and it sounds like an academic strategy you are going to talk about."

"It's no theory, it's very practical."

"OK," said Harley, "what is the Lanchester strategy?"

"I heard about it when I was in Tokyo last year. The bookshops were displaying large numbers of books by one Nobuo Taoko all relating to the Lanchester strategy.

"You, Mike, as a publisher, albeit a fairly new one, will appreciate that Taoko will be a useful addition to anyone's list. His sales are about two million in Japan alone."

"Do you speak Japanese?" asked Cathy.

"Not too well. I know enough words to impress our Japanese customers. But I couldn't read a book."

Harley asked Ashton, "What is the Lanchester strategy and why did the Japanese use a typical English name?"

"It's impossible to condense a most intricate strategy

into a few sentences. You will have to read the book Mike, before you decide whether the Lanchester strategy is worth including. But to answer your query about the name, Lanchester was an engineer – a mathematician. And if that isn't enough he was also an amateur military strategist. His strategy is a combination of our old friend segmentation with a high level of concentration both allied to a typical battlefield strategy."

Cathy said, "This strategy is not for me. It's too complicated."

"You shouldn't say that," said Harley. "We in marketing must have no prior likes or dislikes. We form judgements on knowledge."

"I'm sorry. I'll learn Japanese and read the book."

"Sarcasm will get you nowhere," said Harley, then not wanting to upset Cathy added quickly, "I was only teasing."

"So was I," said Cathy demurely.

Ashton continued. "One aspect of the Lanchester strategy refers to competitors. Roughly it goes like this. Segment the competitor's weakness and strength. Then, like a military commander, attack and keep on attacking that weakness. Concentrate all resources – advertising sales training, PR – on that weakness. Maybe it's a design fault, delivery weakness, service problems; just keep on attacking that segment."

"We did discuss attacking weakness earlier," interrupted Drake.

"I know, but Taoko refers to a complete concentration on one weakness at a time. A good example would be in politics where as soon as the opposition can highlight a weakness or a manufactured weakness in the Prime Minister it never lets that weakness be forgotten. The media may then be their best allies. Winston Churchill acquired the label of a warmonger after the Second World War. The opposition drove that message home so strongly that the public believed it and Labour won the election. We then had weaknesses highlighted in other Prime Ministers: insecurity in one, not caring in another. That is Taoko's message: form a strategy round a weakness and never let go.

"There must be the same segmentation and concentration on your own company's affairs. Attack only one segment of a market at a time; attack the whole market, segment by segment. Concentrate investments on strength in the same way as an army commander does. He rarely reinforces his weak fronts, but gives full backing to the front rolling forward to possible victory. As I mentioned earlier, following segmentation and concentration and military manoeuvres comes mathematical marketing analysis. Over to you, Mike."

Harley said, "It still sounds like another academic theory, but theory or practice, all must be investigated. I'll try to get a translation of Taoko's book."

Drake said, "May I stress a few points, re-cap if you like? A strategy can only be successful if we are aware of whether we get the thumbs up or down from our customers.

1. Forward strategy depends on our ability to identify markets and customer needs. Barratt's housebuilding policy was a good example of that.
2. Ask all managers to identify the strengths and weaknesses in their own divisions; that's one way of learning the truth. Managing directors are often too remote from day-to-day operations to recognise their weaknesses and strengths. They often judge purely on results against budget, without considering whether or not these results could have been improved.
3. Strategy must take into account competitors' reactions to our actions and our reactions to theirs. Their strategy will be based on how they believe we will react to their actions – a new advertising

campaign, sales promotion, new products etc. Knowing this, we should sometimes react in a directly opposite way to their beliefs on our future actions. This can cause them to have misgivings about their own strategy. Here is an example of what I mean.

One of the greatest fights of the past twenty years was between Barry McGuigan and Eusebio Pedroza, for the world featherweight title. McGuigan nearly knocked out his opponent with a right hook and that started the rot. How did that happen? McGuigan's manager had previously sought the advice of Gerald Hayes, who was once Pedroza's sparring partner. Hayes told him that Pedroza would have studied all the videos of McGuigan's fights and would have learned that Barry's favourite punch was with his left hand. Pedroza's strategy would be built around weaving and moving away from that dangerous left. What happened? McGuigan changed his strategy, used his right, knocked down Pedroza – and that was the beginning of the end for him!

4. Never base a strategy on a salesman's generalisations. All strategy must be based on fact."

Cathy said, "I should like to introduce a relatively new strategy. It is franchising, which now applies to computers, car hire, fast foods, printing, plumbing and all kinds of services.

"Our company has considered this strategy for our pest control division and may well make a move in that direction at some time in the future.

"It doesn't apply so much to industrial products but I believe the growth of franchising will exceed all forecasts in the next few years. There's talk of a £10 billion turnover within the next decade. That's worth considering, isn't it?"

"Yes," said Harley, "with one proviso. We covered it

in the first session – research. Many franchisees lose their money riding on the bandwaggon instead of researching into whether the franchise is worth obtaining or whether they have the qualifications and cash to succeed. From a marketing viewpoint if, again, research proves there is a franchise market then that is a strategy well worth considering."

Harley looked at his watch. "Just time for a self questioning quiz."

1. Do we have a knowledge of market size and our share of that market?
2. Do we check to see that we deliver on time? Do we refuse to make excuses if we don't?
3. Do we have a quality strategy?
4. Do we have a packaging strategy?
5. Do we have a discount strategy or are discounts allowed on the spur of the moment? Sudden changes as trade goes up or down – that's always a bad strategy.
6. Do we have a strategy responding immediately to inquiries or requests for quotations?
7. Do we have a communication strategy, letter writing, report writing?
8. Do we have a long-term export strategy?
9. What is our training strategy?
10. What is our research and development strategy?
11. Do we have a time management strategy?
12. Do we have a growth strategy? Should it be inbuilt or by diversification, or both?
13. Do we have a technical support strategy?
14. Do we have a strategy for handling complaints?
15. Do we have a marketing services strategy – publicity brochure designing, direct mail?

8 Personal Research

Lunch was light and short. Afterwards Harley left to make some telephone calls while the others made their way to the lounge.

Over coffee Ashton said to Colin Drake, "Advertising is so far removed from publishing. Do you think Mike will be a successful publisher or is he building the company to sell out?"

Drake shrugged his shoulders. "I have no idea of his plans," he said. "I was one of his clients; incidentally he made such a strong presentation to our board that we ditched our own agency and switched to Harleys. Later we became good friends. Whenever I was in London we met and when I visited New York for the first time he was most helpful.

"He seems too kindly to be outstanding in the advertising field, where dog eats dog for breakfast and knives are stuck in backs regularly."

Hayes smiled. "He wins friends because he is so likeable, but he has one of the shrewdest brains I have come across. And he always plays to win.

"He really is tough, except with women. He was taken for a ride by a New York socialite and her subsequent divorce settlement fleeced him for all he had. But even that hasn't wrinkled his soul. If a man had taken some similar action, in a different way of course, Mike would have set out coldly and clinically to destroy him. He's a great fellow is Mike Harley and a brilliant marketing man. He'll succeed as a book publisher all right as he has succeeded in everything he has done, except marriage. How does he appeal to you, Cathy?"

"Very much, from a business viewpoint of course. I know I am going to get a lot out of our sessions." Then she quickly changed the subject and asked, "What are your special marketing attributes, Ian? We are rightly covering research and strategy, but neither will succeed if marketing managers have closed minds, are not clear thinkers, delegate through fear of making a mistake or lack drive. What makes a good marketing manager?"

Ashton answered, "You are generalising now. You first asked me a personal question and I will reply to that. As you know I was export sales director before I became marketing director. My first thought on receiving my new appointment was of creating a greater sales effort. Our managing director, Hugh Taylor, told me that although I had overall responsibility for sales, I had two main functions. One was to research for new products or so improve our present products that competition was temporarily left behind. The other was to find new markets and licensing opportunities.

"I also received a directive from Hugh. He told me that I could rely on him to help keep production cost down and to make the investments essential to growth. But it was my job to keep down marketing costs. I accepted that challenge.

"Marketeers are notoriously big spenders unless they have self-control. Nearly every marketing manager could cut 10 per cent off his costs; so much expenditure in marketing is not cost-effective. Every new plan, every suggestion, every idea made to a marketing director is an invitation to spend more money. He is the controller of the cash and he has the authority to spend it. He is the one who fights for increased advertising and argues with his managing director that he should spend more on exhibitions or foreign travel. He may well argue for larger cars for his sales force or other employees. In fact he increases expenditure everywhere. That's why he has to have great self-control. My attributes therefore are product innovation, finding new markets and being able to keep costs down. The marketing manager who is really cost conscious is in line for promotion. There are so few of them about."

"Are you cost conscious?" asked Cathy.

"Yes, I am."

"So you must be in line for promotion. You will be managing director one day."

"Happily yes," said Ashton surprisingly.

And they all knew the job was being lined up for him.

Then Ashton said, "Now Cathy, it's your turn. Tell us what makes you tick. Why you are outstanding as a marketing director?"

"You're being very flattering," said Cathy. "I wish I was outstanding, but I am good I admit that. I believe that too many marketing directors are so involved with top level management that they forget the selling function and even distance themselves from sales management. They remember the old tag, that a marketing manager is only a salesman with a different title and want no part of that. But what's the use of finding a new export market if the export salesman cannot close orders? What use is a big advertising campaign if salesmen don't enthusiastically scuttle round to customers making sure they are well stocked? The marketing director must delegate authority to the sales manager, but delegation does not mean total passing of the buck. Too many marketing directors when asked for advice by their sales manager tend to reply 'That's your baby, you decide'. This is wrong.

"The marketing director should go into the field now and again however large his company, otherwise he will lose touch with the sales force. It's not only the sales force who need motivating it's the sales managers as well.

In my case we have four sales managers covering our various divisions, ten regional sales managers and many more area managers. I hold sales meetings with the sales managers every month and with the regional sales managers every three months.

"Too many men and women promoted to marketing director become desk bound – they should be outward bound. Then they will find ideas for new products and new markets. Salesmanship is my main strength."

She spoke with such verve and enthusiasm that Bruce Hayes clapped and said, "Cathy you can convince anyone about anything. But a marketing manager shouldn't be single-minded. He, or she, must be multi-disciplined and be able to give advice, judgements, decisions on all aspects of marketing. That, I believe, is my strength. At our management meetings the atmosphere is quite electric; our managers are clear thinkers and enthusiastic about all aspects of life assurance; but a lack of knowledge is not acceptable. Therefore, while agreeing with Cathy that selling is all-important, I have made myself learn more about other disciplines. I can hold my own with the experts on direct mail and public relations and have a good all-round knowledge of accountancy. No actuary can blind me with his science. Talking advertising strategy is second nature to me. I shan't look a bloody fool, even when the computer boys get going in their own language. So, three cheers for the multi-disciplined marketing manager!"

Cathy agreed. "You're right, Bruce. But most of us have one outstanding discipline which we have really mastered. Selling is mine."

"Yes," said Bruce. "I'm trying to think what I'm really best at."

Colin Drake said, "I believe that above all I'm in people management which means I put people first, a quality every manager pays lip service to but very few carry out even the first principles. My main job is getting along with and motivating people. How else does one get the best out of associates and employees, advertising agents, overseas customers, chain store buyers?

"So many marketing directors, managing directors, company chairmen are quite cold fish really and as I said only pay lip service to putting people first. Possibly they do when things go right, but they rarely blame themselves first if things go wrong. I do. We have four separate companies each with its own marketing director and managing director. None of them wants interference from headquarters. It's my job to be seen by them to be fair, willing to listen and knowledgeable. That's what they look for at our meetings. I agree with all the qualities listed by Bruce, and in Mike's determination to win, but my priority is people management."

"Good for you," said Ashton.

"Can I make a final point? We marketing people depend so much on our managing directors. If, like mine, they are forward looking, then marketing has a priority. If, however, they are financiers, engineers, economists, then marketing will often take a back seat. I'm afraid that too many of our leading companies stand still or go backwards because their managing directors do not realise the importance of marketing, although they make a pretence of doing so."

"A final word from me, too," said Hayes. "As marketing managers we should also consider the managing director's viewpoint. We tend only to see things from a marketing point of view and that too is wrong. He has to consider world economics, political issues, social problems, investments . . . which is why we should try to be multi-disciplined, so that we can see the managing director's viewpoint when he decides against us."

Drake looked at his watch. "Ten minutes to go. Now let me put my people management to the test:

"Cathy, will you join me for a walk in the garden?" He stood up, and she joined him, linking her arm in his.

9 Telephone Selling

The afternoon meeting began with Harley.

"Although we decided not to cover salesmanship in depth, we did decide to incorporate a telephone strategy – mainly directed towards selling because it has now become an important marketing strategy. It offers many benefits, some of which are:

vetting applicants, rather than wasting time writing letters or granting unnecessary interviews
researching
making appointments for salesmen
building lists for direct mail
checking retail stock
following up a letter request for information
following up enquiries
subscription renewals
seeking dealers, distributors, agents
checking advertising
collecting accounts
selling extras
reminding buyers of new product promotions
contacting old customers to check if they are in the market again to buy and
direct selling.

"Are there any more telephoning objectives you would like to add to that list?"

Cathy answered, "Yes. I would want marketing

managers to be more aware of the goodwill they lose through bad telephone management. Recently I gave an order to a famous food store. I won't name them because there's no point in getting someone into trouble when the fault lies with management. Usually that store delivers food within twenty-four hours, certainly forty-eight at the most. Nothing had been delivered after seven days, so I telephoned to ask the reason. The receptionist put me through to the order department. I was told that I should be speaking to the despatch department. The despatch clerk said I wanted the accounts department and the accounts department assistant put me back to the order department.

"I was then told that it was all the fault of a new computer and the delivery would now be made quickly. But nothing happened for four more days. So I wrote to the general manager. Next morning I was telephoned, apologies were offered and I was assured that delivery would be made by return and that's what did happen.

"The excuse: my order had been mislaid. This kind of thing happens all the time. But surely it is unforgiveable when management does not ensure that those who answer the telephone have enough understanding of who does what in the organisation to enable a customer to be transferred to the correct department and person who can deal with a query. No marketing manager should ever use the excuse 'you can't get good staff these days'. That is an admission of management weakness."

When Cathy stopped talking Harley asked for any further contributions on telephone usage.

Ashton said, "My pet hate is the failure of receptionists to monitor a call. Often when I telephone someone the receptionist cannot put me through immediately, maybe a line is engaged or that person is away from the office. I will be told to hold on. Nothing happens. I still hold on. Still nothing happens. But that call should be monitored. The receptionist should ask me every minute or two, 'Do you still want to hold on? I am sorry the line is still engaged,' or 'Would you like us to call you back?' or 'Would you like to call later?'

"This is all very basic stuff but so many telephone problems would be solved if only management would continually check on the way their own staff are using the telephones."

Harley said, "Now for my pet hate. It is the person who wants to speak to me and asks his secretary or receptionist to contact me first. I then have to hold on until Mr or Mrs Caller deigns to speak to me. This has to be acceptable from those who buy from us but not from anyone else. It is so pompous for Mr *X* to say to his secretary 'Get Mr *Y* on the phone'. Callers should dial their own number on their own phones and waste their own time holding on, rather than waste somebody else's time.

"Often I have held on for a caller only to be told by a receptionist or secretary a few minutes later, 'I'm sorry, he must have left his office. I'll call you back later.' That is unforgiveable!"

Bruce Hayes said, "I agree with every word you say, Mike. But I should like to add a rider, if I may.

"It's this: Everyone in a company is involved in selling. Goodwill creating is indirect selling. The accountant, the distribution manager, the office manager, clerks, typists, draughtsmen – all, when they use the telephone, can make or mar goodwill.

"The secretary who speaks abruptly to a caller daring to ask to speak to her boss may be affecting company goodwill. The boss who shows his authority by speaking in a peremptory manner loses business. Possibly worst of all are those responsible for receiving enquiries over the telephone.

"Recently, I read a very good advertisement by a car manufacturer setting out the advantages of buying their make of car. At the foot of the advertisement was a line which read: 'To receive immediate service, telephone our hotline'. I telephoned and asked for a brochure to be sent. Nothing happened for fourteen days. Can you believe that? I telephoned again and again nothing happened for the next four or five days. Eventually the brochure was received, but by this time I had lost interest.

"The advertiser must have known that anyone reading the words 'hot line' would assume that they would receive information by return. Yet another management weakness, in not laying down a rigorous system which would result in enquiries receiving immediate attention."

Harley said, "I do hope every reader of the book will study Bruce's story carefully and ask himself the question: 'Does this weakness apply to my organisation?'

"Bruce is certainly the most experienced of all of us in this sphere of marketing. Insurance and assurance people live by telephone usage, they sell on the phone, they make appointments by phone and all their calls are treated as forerunners of business.

"Bruce has told me that Atlantis Assurance have their own separate training organisation which all members of the staff must attend. They also offer training to outside organisations. Bruce will not mind my saying that there are two reasons for this:

"The first is to keep their top-rate team of training instructors fully occupied. The second is that all those attending the courses will be indirectly motivated to use Atlantis when considering assurance.

"Bruce has taken part in many sessions, including telephone selling. He has some notes with him and has agreed to give us extracts from this course. So over to you, Bruce."

"Before I begin I must apologise. What you are about to hear will sound more like a lecture than the basis for a discussion. The reason is that it is a lecture, lifted straight from our telephone selling course. So, on with the show!

"It cannot be over-emphasised that if the product and the strategy are right only one gimmick is needed to succeed in marketing – efficiency. The majority of companies, including our own, are efficient in some areas and not so good in others. We have to strive to eradicate marketing weaknesses. Some believe that it is enough to have the right product at the right price. It is not! There are many other facets of a company's activities which help salesmen to close more orders. We are discussing just one of these facets, telephone usage, which is a great weakness in most companies.

"I'll begin with the first lesson in our course. It is the need to learn a set telephone presentation, whether by a receptionist following an incoming call, or a member of the sales team making a call with the object of getting an order. There must be carefully worked out steps to the ultimate aim – goodwill, a decision, or a sale. You will find that the formula laid down at our courses will apply to all areas of telephone usage.

"Mike told me that there will only be space in the book to cover a telephone sales presentation, but the step-by-step approach to the sales presentation needs only the slightest adaptation to make it suitable for any type of call.

"If we consider some of the disadvantages of telephone selling I believe it will then become clearer as to why we must have a motivated presentation. The telephone salesman cannot show shimmering materials, or bullet-proof glass, or computers activated by a voice; neither can the receiver of the call be won over by a warm friendly smile, honest blue eyes, or a confidence-building appearance.

"The telephone user can only win over a difficult customer, soothe an irate caller, or persuade a reluctant recipient of a call to say 'yes', by the words he or she uses. The telephone sales person is, in fact, a processor of words. The better the words the greater the act of persuasion, but that doesn't mean using longer words than necessary. The objective is to use time and time is so important over the telephone.

"Why say, for example, 'participate', when 'share' will do? Why 'approximate'? 'About' is enough. Why 'commence' when 'begin' will do? 'A large number of' only means 'many'. 'In a majority of instances' is covered by 'mostly'. 'I am of the opinion' means 'I believe'. 'Now' is preferable to 'the present time'. And never use such clichés as 'in this day and age', 'as of now', 'at this moment in time'.

"How many will take the trouble to think of word power on the lines I suggested? How many will remain inefficient by relying solely on their own vocabulary?

"After we get the words right we can move on to the building of a sales presentation. There are only five main steps, but each has to be elaborated:

1. The opening.
2. Creation of interest. One and two are closely allied.
3. A main benefit to receiver.
4. A subsidiary benefit to receiver.
5. A motivating close.

"Let us go through the formula step by step. There is a choice when considering the opening you will use. It could be based on one of the following:

a fact
a question
a topical subject
to arouse curiosity
a reference from a friend or business associate
an advertising campaign

a TV campaign
an exhibition
a letter
a gift
fear
a service
a promotional campaign
a bargain offer.

Here are some examples of various openings:

Question opening to a travel agent:

'Mr John Brown?'

'Yes'. (Then repeat his name.)

'Mr Brown, this is Tom Smith of the Decorative Flower Company. Do you find that a high proportion of women make the bookings for family holidays?'

'Yes.'

'Mr Brown, then a bowl of our colourful and appealing artificial flowers placed in your window would attract attention. They are marvellously real eye catchers . . .'

Here is a reference opening:

'Mr Arthur White?'

'Yes.'

'Mr White, can you spare me a few moments?'

'Yes.'

'This is Tom Smith of Direct Supplies Ltd. Recently we were able to make drastic reductions in the cost of carbon paper for your friend Mr Lever of Lever & Jenkins. He told me he felt sure you would want to make similar savings and suggested that I telephone you . . .'

Now for a fear opening:

'Mr Green?'

'Yes.'

> 'Mr Green, this is Tom Smith of Causeway Garages. It's just ten months since you purchased your car from us. When you called in for petrol the other day our attendant noticed that the treads on your tyres were wearing. You know, Mr Green, sometimes we only discover a tyre problem when it's too late . . .'

Then there is the bargain opening:

> 'Mr Blue?'
>
> 'Yes.'
>
> 'Mr Blue, this is Tom Smith of Apex Toiletries. My reason for calling you is that new price schedules are coming into effect on the first of next month. As an old and loyal customer I wanted to give you the special opportunity of placing an order now for your forward requirements . . .'

"We then tell those at the course to study the list of suggested approaches and to ally each one of them to their product or service. We advise them to seek new openings from time to time, because selling is not static. A company may launch a new advertising campaign or a new product. Trial and error may prove that the factual opening is better than a reference opening. All openings, however, must arouse immediate interest. If it works, it's right.

"The opening is followed by the main and subsidiary benefits, when these rhetorical questions are put.

"When buying a house, do we buy it because of the depth of its foundation, the glazed bricks on the outside walls, the solidity of structure? Or do we buy because of the pride we will feel in our new home, future capital appreciation, the warmth of the central heating, and the easy-work kitchen?

"When buying a new line in packet soups, does the caterer buy because of the freshness of the vegetables used, the modern conversion plant, the new airtight packaging, or because he believes that the new packet soups will please his customers and increase his margin or profit?

"The answers are obvious. People buy for personal benefit, to satisfy a human need. The main consideration of a space buyer contemplating advertising in a magazine is: Will it bring in enough inquiries to make the advertisement profitable? A secondary benefit might be pride in the impact the advertisement will make on his customers. A third benefit, the praise he may receive from his managing director for the success of the campaign.

"If a telephone salesman selling space were trying to close the order with that buyer he would, therefore, make his main benefit *profit*, and his secondary benefit *satisfaction* or *pride* or to *gain praise*.

"In the industrial world, the main buying reason is nearly always gain of money or saving of money, but there is a wide variety of subsidiary reasons. In telephone selling there is usually only time to give the main benefit and one subsidiary benefit.

"The following buying motivators are not all-embracing, but they will cover 80 to 90 per cent of buying reasons. I'll list them in no particular order:

gain of money
saving money
satisfaction of caution
satisfaction of pride
to avoid effort
comfort
sentiment
pleasure
health
to satisfy hunger
utility
envy
love
to obtain security

to obtain more leisure
to satisfy ego
to protect family
to attract the opposite sex
to gain popularity
to gain praise
safety
to possess beautiful objects
to impress others."

Hayes invited questions and then continued. "The next step in building the sales presentation is company and product analysis.

"Sometimes it is essential to prove a need first, but always a need must be turned into a want. Before this objective can be reached we must define the main reasons for the prospect or customer wanting a product or service.

"This want will stem from the benefits which he will derive from the product, reinforced by the confidence he has in the company and its ability to maintain quality, promises of delivery etc.

"First must come company analysis to discover benefit:

Is the company the leader in its field. If so, why?
When was it established?
What are its future plans?
Where are its factories?
How many personnel are engaged in research?
Who is head of the research division? What is his background?
Is the managing director known in any sphere other than his own?

"Next comes product analysis:

Is it new?

How long has it been on the market?
Is it derived from a successful predecessor?
Why is it ahead of competitor's products?
How is it constructed?
Why is it less expensive?
Why is it more expensive?
Has it prestige value?
Is it packed in some special way?
Is it covered by a long-term guarantee?
Does it hold the greater share of the market? If so, why?
Is demand increasing?
Can extra rapid service be carried out?
Can it be adapted specially for a customer?
Is it a novelty?
Will it sell all the year round?

"The product analysis must be in depth and only when all the benefits are listed can the telephone salesman begin to work out his own presentation.

"The salesman knows that his prospects are not interested in technicalities, but only the benefits they derive from them. He therefore reminds himself that he must always express benefits in terms of buyers' interests. In order not to forget this fact during a presentation he uses three link words: 'which means that'. This is how he would use the link words:

> 'It is silent in operation Mr Brown, *which means that* the health of your staff will not be affected by noise.'
> 'It stops condensation Mr Smith, *which means that* you will save on decorations, cease living in a damp atmosphere and avoid discoloration of furnishings.'

"Always remember the words 'which means that'.

"But a statement, however good it may be, need not increase the chance of a sale. Why? Because we do not know:

(a) if the prospect has heard us
(b) if he has understood us
(c) if he agrees with us.

"We therefore have to adopt a technique of making positive statements and asking positive questions which will evoke 'yes' responses. When we have our prospect's agreement, we know that we can continue with our presentation.

"The telephone salesman will therefore prepare a number of questions to which he is certain of getting a 'yes' response.

'You do agree that advertising on the packet is good advertising, don't you Mr Smith?'
'You would like to increase your profit margin, wouldn't you Mrs White?'
'If you could cut costs by 5 per cent right away you would want to start immediately, wouldn't you?'
'Mr Brown, you wouldn't like to take any risks for one day longer than you need, so I am sure you would like to be covered right away, wouldn't you?'
'You do risk losing custom when you are out of stock, don't you?'
'A series of advertisements would bring far better results against cost, I am sure you agree with that, Mr Johnson?'

"So far we have won attention and created interest with our opening and we have given a main and subsidiary benefit. Now we must get a decision to close the order.

"Often a play or musical fails in a London theatre after a provincial run. Then the excuses flow from the producer, director, actors and actresses: 'We opened at the wrong time'; 'The weather was against us'; 'The critics panned us unfairly'; 'We were affected by the strike.'

"These excuses make no allowance for the fact that other shows managed to carry on in spite of these difficulties.

"When a production fails the reason can usually be traced to mistakes in judgement. The playwright would not accept changes; others involved refused to accept criticism; the actors and actresses were badly cast. . . . Problems during the provincial run were waved aside as being of no consequence: 'It will be all right on the night!' But the show was doomed to failure from the beginning. Would the playwright ever admit this? Would the actor agree that he was inaudible to the back row? Would the producer believe that the play which had a special message couldn't find an audience who wanted to listen to that message?

"The failure was not due to any sudden change in the weather, or a strike, or even the critics who panned it. Many shows have succeeded in spite of such criticism. The play failed way back.

"Sales are never lost at the last moment. The mistakes are made much earlier. All telephone salesmen should write on a card: 'I do not lose orders because of my weak closing techniques. I lose orders because my presentation is not good enough'.

"That is the first lesson to be learned if more orders are to be obtained. The old selling axiom that 'a good sale closes itself' is still true. Sometimes a buyer, even although he is well sold, is still hesitant and there are many ways of leading him into saying 'Yes'.

"You must always ask for the order, but if you fail you must leave an opening so that your next call will be welcome. On making your second call be positive and assume that the decision is in your favour. Never ask, 'Have you made up your mind?' Take up a point from the previous call and continue from that point.

"When the order is closed ring off quickly to cement confidence:

'I'll telephone you again when it is delivered.'
'I'll make sure it is delivered on time.'
'You will be delighted when it is installed.'

"When selling consumer goods the salesman will close quickly on each line as it is offered.

"Now, how do we ask for the order? The direct request can be made:

'I take it that you want one.'
'Will you give me the order?'

"You might win, but you might precipitate the clicking of the receiver as it is placed back on the cradle. The prospect's 'No' is so final. Far better than putting a direct question is to offer the prospect alternatives.

'Would you prefer a gross or two gross with the special discount?'

'It could be installed in the window facing south or the one facing east. Which is your preference?'

'Would you prefer our cleaning staff to arrive early in the morning or after you have closed in the evenings?'

"If an indecisive reply is received to any of these alternatives, the salesman has still not lost the order or command of the situation. He can continue selling. Often, however, the alternative close is linked with other methods of finalising the presentation. These can be closes within their own right, but when the buyer needs an extra nudge, use the 'alternative close'. Here are some proven closes.

"The 'concession close' – When selling consumer goods, special promotions and concessions are usually part of the sales presentation. There are occasions when a salesman can grant a concession which is not allowed to all of his customers: extra discount, longer credit, special deliveries, thirteen for twelve, a free service, a refund guarantee.

"Many telephone salesmen give the concession at the opening but this is wrong. The rule is: sell as if you did not have the concession. The order might close easily and you have no need to give away some of your company's profits. It is when the order is proving difficult to close that the concession can have real weight.

"There is also the 'summary close'. In telephone selling the presentation is so short that the majority of prospects will retain the main points in their mind, but there is always the buyer who only half listens and even gives 'yes' responses automatically. For those buyers, the telephone salesman summarises the main features and benefits of his product and then asks for the order. The summary close is sometimes called the 'reminder' close.

"The 'verbal proof story close' is similar to the reference opening. It is a confidence builder and can be most helpful when selling to a timid buyer. The telephone salesman concludes his presentation with a success story involving another customer's satisfaction.

"Then there is closing on a minor point. This is part assumptive close – which only means that the salesman *assumes* he is going to get the order and is therefore more positive – and part alternative close. The telephone salesman will say:

'You do agree, Mr Brown, that you prefer a remote control with the unit, don't you?'

'Mr Smith, we deliver Thursday. Would that be all right for you?'

'As it is a present, Miss Jones, would you like it specially gift wrapped?'

"The telephone salesman must assume that if the prospect agrees on the minor point he or she is ready to place the order.

"It is always fear which stops prospects from buying – fear of making a mistake, fear of a reprimand from higher authority, fear of spending too much money, fear of loss of security, fear of what a wife or husband will say, fear of over-stocking, fear of being talked into an order.

"You must calm their fears by closing in a positive

manner. Until the sale is closed the salesman is a conversationalist. Only when the order is finalised is he a salesman. An attempt must always be made to close an order or get a decision. The fact that someone has made the enquiry means that they are interested. Even if an order cannot be booked over the telephone, the extra benefit of the service or product must still be stressed.

"In business today there is little to choose between many similar products or services. The dynamic efficient company will always get more than its share of the market, because it will give that extra service – a service so rarely given by many companies, both large and small.

"That extra service ensures that everyone who telephones your company is given a warm and friendly welcome, is dealt with efficiently and courteously and is made to feel that the call is not an intrusion on someone's time, but a very welcome event.

" 'May I help you?' must convey the message: 'I really do want to help you!'

"And that," concluded Hayes, "is what is meant by a telephone selling strategy, which should be a part of every marketing strategy."

Everyone applauded. Harley shook Bruce Hayes' hand and as the tea trolley arrived he said, "I think you deserve a break, Bruce!"

10 The Corbett Strategy

The tea break had just commenced, when a porter arrived with a message for Harley. He glanced at it and hurried out of the room. Susan Clifford was waiting for him in the lounge, but before he could greet her he was intercepted by an apologetic head receptionist who explained how the earlier message that Miss Clifford had left had inadvertently gone astray.

Harley accepted the apology and crossed the lounge to greet a flustered looking Susan. Her immediate words were, "I had to come! I hope I did right, but . . ."

"Don't worry, Susan," said Harley. "You wouldn't be here unless the matter was urgent and important. I'll order tea and join you in a few minutes." He beckoned a waitress and organised tea and cakes, then walked slowly and thoughtfully back to the meeting room. There he was greeted by noisy chatter mixed with the clatter of cups and saucers.

He said, "You've had a long day. The sun is shining and the birds are twittering, so let's enjoy the great outdoors until dinner. We can get in three full sessions tomorrow. OK?"

Everyone agreed. There followed a brief discussion about the following day's sessions and, leaving the team to finish their tea and cakes, Harley hurried back to Susan Clifford.

"I rang earlier," she began, "but . . ."

"I know," interrupted Harley, "but tell me the bad

news. You wouldn't have driven eighty miles to give me good news. What's happened?"

Tea arrived and Susan waited until the waitress had left before speaking again. During that short interval Harley noticed that her previous flushed complexion had now turned a greyish colour and her lipstick didn't quite cover the contour of her lips. He smiled at her encouragingly and she began.

"This morning Kenneth Jason called me into his office. When I arrived Clive Chapman was also there and instinctively I felt something was wrong. Kenneth, as you know, has always been most kind to me and although Clive and I have had our differences we have always been good friends. They looked so grave and serious that I thought Kenneth was going to give me the sack."

Harley restrained his impatience. He wanted Susan to get on with the news, not to relate the embellishments to the story.

She continued. "I know this will upset you. It certainly upset me. Kenneth offered me a far better paid job with Brooke & Dean."

Harley's mouth tightened. It was the next move he had been expecting from Corbett, but he didn't think Susan would be involved and he hadn't expected it to happen so soon.

Susan began sobbing. Harley had never known how to handle a 'sobber'. He wanted to walk away, or to shout 'For God's sake stop crying and get on with the story!' He did neither. He patted her hand and said, "Take your time."

She took her time. After a minute or so she dabbed her eyes with a tissue, straightened her shoulders, and said, "I'm sorry, but I can't stand deceit. I was so shocked when Kenneth made the offer that I was quite speechless. Kenneth didn't appreciate my feelings and what he actually said to me was: 'This will come as a pleasant surprise to you, Susan, I know, but we all have our futures to think of and Clive and I are so happy that you can share your future with us'."

She stopped for a moment to wipe her lips with the tissue clenched in her hand, then tucking it into her sleeve she went on. "Honestly, Mike, my mind almost stopped working. I couldn't grasp the situation at all, so I blurted out, 'Are they taking us over?' Kenneth said, 'Not at all, we're almost taking them over.' And he and Clive both laughed very heartily."

She went on to explain once more how upset she was; how, for the first time, she had noticed the bloodshot eyes of Kenneth Jason and Clive's rather cunning expression. It occurred to Harley that, in her mind, Susan was editing a romantic novel. He let her run on a few minutes longer then said, "Susan, I have to get back to the meeting. Please tell me the facts as briefly as you can."

"I'm sorry," Susan apologised. "Kenneth said he had been approached by a head hunter – one of those people, you know, who act behind the scenes to entice managers away from their jobs."

"I know," Harley said gently.

"And this head hunter told him that the position with Brooke & Dean as joint managing director was open for him at a very high salary plus a share of the profits. Kenneth explained how later he had been interviewed by the great Mr Corbett himself and had accepted the position. He said Mr Corbett had also offered very good terms to Clive, to me and to our London and Scottish representatives. Clive would become marketing director and I should be joint chief editor. I couldn't believe my ears. I'm not used to that sort of thing . . ."

Harley said, "Please don't worry, Susan. Everything will be OK."

She looked sceptically at him, but continued with her story: "Kenneth said Corbett had offered to take us over and had been badly misled by you, Mike. He also said that he wanted Harley's because of the high reputation of the directors. That I couldn't believe, much as I respect our directors. After all they have a very good man in Reg Panton whom I've met several times. But Kenneth is no fool and he believes the truth is that Corbett has been affronted by you and tycoons do not like being affronted! Kenneth believes Corbett has decided to make things so difficult for us that he'll be able to buy us out at a bargain price. But this is the awful part: Kenneth and Clive both said they have no faith in you; that you'll probably sell out later anyway in spite of your promises and maybe leave us all stranded. Kenneth said that was why we should make our move now, rather than perhaps be discarded later."

Harley asked, "But how will the directors of Brooke & Dean react?"

"Corbett told Kenneth that they were very happy. He said Reg Panton and his colleagues didn't believe they were losing anything, only gaining associates to help build the business and share their problems.

"All those approached are old servants of Harley's; men who have professed loyalty first to your father and uncle and later to you. Do you remember at your first meeting, how all the staff stood up and applauded you and promised their full backing? They have always claimed with pride that they are part of the Harley family. How could such men take actions like that, when you are trying to rebuild the business? Where is their honour?"

"Does honour still exist in business? I think money takes precedence these days!"

"Not with me! But then I believe that women are more loyal than men anyway."

"Thank you, Susan. But are you sure you're doing the right thing by staying with me?"

"I wouldn't go with them for any money."

Harley said, "Thank you again. When are they leaving?"

"This week."

"What!"

"Yes. Corbett has agreed to cover all costs should you insist on them forfeiting pay instead of working out their notice, which they didn't think you would want them to do anyway."

"And when do they intend to tell me?"

"They haven't the courage to tell you, they're such cowards! They're going to write you letters. You'll receive them here some time this week."

Neither spoke for a few moments, while Susan refilled the teacups. Harley saw Cathy James entering the lounge. He attracted Cathy's attention, much to Susan's surprise, and beckoned her over. Harley introduced Cathy to Susan and invited her to join them. He quickly told her Susan's news and then, realising Susan's bewilderment, explained that Cathy was an old friend and he had already discussed with her the implications of Corbett's ownership of the Browser Bookshops.

Harley continued. "We both agreed that it was Corbett's first step in knocking out Harley's and that his next step would be to try and attract away our key staff. It's a strategy constantly used in the advertising, magazine publishing and newspaper world."

Cathy said to Susan, "I admire your attitude."

"There's nothing to admire," Susan cut in sharply. "Wrongdoers should be punished, but those who do what is right and honest, which should be natural to all of us, shouldn't require praise."

Sensing her antagonism Cathy went on quickly, "I do so agree, Susan. I was only trying to say the right thing. I should have kept quiet, I'm sorry!"

Immediately Susan softened. "I'm afraid I'm a bit uptight still. You'll have to forgive me."

The altercation over, Susan drank her tea and then, as

if she had received an inspiration from heaven said, "Why don't you telephone Mr Prewett and see if he can't get an injunction to stop that Corbett man enticing our people away? If it's granted by a judge it could take weeks before the case comes to court and in the meantime our directors' names will be mud in the trade. That wouldn't do them any good!"

Harley shook his head. "If that were possible, head hunters would be out of business. There's only a case for court action if there is a breach of contract. And Harley's never gave their employees contracts. If an employee does not give the statutory notice, an injunction can be obtained against him or the company about to employ him, but even if we could get an injunction, it wouldn't help. I shouldn't want them to continue at Harley's and, for that matter, neither would you, Susan. So we'd be no better off."

Cathy said, "The loss of two salesmen will lose Harley's some business in the short term and Jason and Chapman's defection will only cause hardship in the short term, until they are replaced. Isn't that right?"

"I'm afraid not," said Susan. "Our leading authors are very close to Kenneth. He's always ignored the lesser authors, but really fusses over those who are highly profitable to us. Also the literary agents know him so well that they will give him first refusals, now that they know he has cash resources behind him. And Clive, too, is on very friendly terms with some of the biggest book buyers in the country. His story will be that Harley's are in a bad way and it was only fair to himself and the authors to move on. Also, it's very difficult to find replacements.

"Who would want to join Harley's if they thought we were going under? Everything's stacked against us! Harley's was such a wonderful name and the brothers were such splendid people."

"And what about me?" said Mike with a smile.

"I was so sure you'd follow in their footsteps. What are we going to do?"

Harley patted her arm. "Don't worry, Susan," he said. "It's not what we're going to do, it's what I'm already doing that will solve our problems."

11 New Ideas for New Products

Opening the Wednesday morning session Harley did not feel tired, although he had had only three hours' sleep the previous night.

Following his meeting with Susan he had made several telephone calls and then driven to London. He returned by minicab, arriving at Pellew Grange after 1 a.m., well satisfied with his evening's work.

Bruce Hayes was the first to speak. "We decided that the first two sessions this morning would be on 'product strategy' and 'pricing strategy', but don't you think it would be better if they were replaced by 'advertising' and 'promotions or direct marketing?' These subjects can be so absorbing, even exciting. It's difficult, in my opinion, to raise much enthusiasm for 'product strategy'. After all, our objective must be to hold the attention of the reader and we can best do that by introducing meaty sessions early on."

Ashton interrupted. "Sorry, Bruce, but I disagree. As Cathy said, we can have the finest products, but they won't sell themselves in today's competitive markets. Conversely we can have the finest salesmen, but they won't close many orders if the products are out of date, or new products to fill customer needs are not introduced. In marketing there should be no one section more important than any other. They're all integrated into a unified marketing plan. The same applies to strategic pricing. Get it wrong and profits may fall, or advantage won't be taken of a temporary sellers' market, or sales will be hard to come by. To my mind product and pricing strategies are vitally important, possibly more important than advertising. It's no use advertising the wrong product!"

Harley said, "Bruce, in assurance you do have a product – the policy – and the terms and conditions of policies change continually to meet current needs, but your product is not quite the same from a marketing point of view as Ian's, Colin's or Cathy's.

"I agree with Ian. And there is another important point: the book should be read by non-marketing managers. The importance of research and development should be impressed on them, as should product development and pricing. To use Colin's phrase, all managers these days must be multi-disciplined."

Bruce held up his hand. "I surrender!" he said. "Carry on with product strategy."

Harley smiled. "Thanks, Bruce. Ian, the subject's right up your street; will you begin?"

Ashton stood up and said, "First of all, when considering product strategy there is always a danger of attempting to cover too much ground.

"The advice of sales managers and salesmen, backroom boys, and even managing directors, is to add to the range – to try to cover every conceivable customer need. Imagine if Ford decided to make a range of cars, from minis to Rolls Royces, with a Porsche look-alike in between. This is the worst kind of product strategy.

"I'm sure you would find it so, Colin, if you listened to and agreed with all the demands you receive for new products. You'd have two hundred or more different varieties of biscuit to compete with all those on the shelves."

Colin Drake nodded his agreement and Ashton went on. "In my field of engineering there is always someone succeeding with products similar to ours, with which we are urged to compete. If we make twenty different sizes, someone will demand another ten. If we finish in five different colours there will always be a request for another, and another, and so on. And, of course, there are always units to meet special situations.

"The right policy should be completely the reverse – a good dictum being constantly to study the range to see what can be omitted and only to add to it after the most careful research. Sometimes it's better to concentrate product strategy on a small but highly profitable group of customers or, perhaps, one section of the market, rather than aim at covering every aspect of customer needs. One certain recipe for failure is to have too many products chasing too few customers. Concentration, as that Japanese author said, can be the guide to a successful product strategy."

"May I interrupt?" said Colin Drake. "Although I agree with cutting poor performance products from a range, we must always keep up the pressure with the bestsellers. Salesmen and even customers quickly tire of products, even those with household names. Buyers are continually being tempted away by specious claims from competitors, particularly in the retail distribution field. We marketing managers must, now and again, introduce incentives for both salesmen and customers to maintain salesmen's enthusiasm and product loyalty."

Ashton said, "You're right, of course! There are exceptions to every rule, but we have to be careful that the range is not extended unnecessarily or marketed beyond its time. The great persuaders who want us to introduce additions to the range, or refuse to remove marginal profit makers from the range, refer continually to 'contribution' – that is, contribution to overheads. Those who advocate this 'contribution' approach claim that the 'contribution' assists other products to be more profitable. This is nearly always a fallacy. There are additional costs which few take into consideration: time taken by selling, packaging, debt-collecting, worrying, additional publicity material. Time is a general management shortage and must be used to the best advantage, which means selling products which are profitable in their own right, not those which sell in small numbers but make an apparent contribution.

"Now I'll switch to another factor: products will always cost more than anticipated. We must bear this in mind. When the true costs are known they always turn out to be higher than the original 'guesstimate'. This has been the cause of many small businesses going bust.

"I would like to talk at length about research and development, but I feel that someone else should give their views on product strategy first."

"I will," answered Hayes. "I'd like to make some points which have been drilled into me for years and which I now try to drill into others.

"In the consumer field, to achieve a short-term success is a tactic which can be self-destructive. For example, heavy advertising can be to the detriment of other products in a range. Such advertising may only bring short-term gains unless the product does have advantages over competitors' and consumers continue to buy after the heavy advertising has stopped. Only when convinced of consumer acceptance of a product should the short-term benefits of heavy advertising be considered. The same applies to special promotions, discounts and other incentives.

"Millions of pounds are lost by pushing products which only have an advertising gimmick appeal. The customer will quickly desert for, possibly, a lower priced 'own label' product. We know that most new products fail in spite of test marketing and one of the reasons is that we marketing people are so apt to believe our own advertising claims.

"Long-term strategy in the consumer field means a gradual build up of customer loyalty. We expect too much from short-term drives and promotions. Always think ahead is the best strategy.

"My next point is: Avoid changing the formula of winning products. This happened in the detergent market, when a new formula was introduced which affected the skin. That product had to be dropped, quickly. Coca Cola is another example of wrongly tampering with product acceptance. Sometimes it's better to introduce a new product rather than radically alter an old one. So remember, don't tamper with consumer acceptance.

"Another question we have to ask is not what makes people buy, but why do some people buy a product while others ignore it? Why do some like and some dislike? What are the 'dislikers' objecting to? To find out is also first-class product strategy. It may show why a product which once sold well is no longer being accepted by the majority.

"Because exporting is a priority, there is a problem in the consumer field. What appeals to one set of consumers at home may not appeal to a similar set abroad. Export product strategy must therefore be considered as a separate function from home product strategy and research should be instigated to discover consumer likes and dislikes in each country.

"Finally, always consult an expert before using brand names worldwide. Because a product has a popular trade name in its home market doesn't mean that it won't annoy, amuse, or come up against local byelaws in a foreign country. There are company brand name advisory consultants whose help should be sought. They are very good at their work."

Ashton turned to Cathy. "Wouldn't you like to say something first?"

"No thanks. I'm quite happy listening to you."

"Thank you. I was only being polite. Back then to my favourite subject: research and development.

"No company can expect future growth without such a department. In the smaller engineering businesses the owner usually has a back room where he works on new product developments, but most medium-sized to large organisations rely on the R & D division, not only for correcting major faults but also to improve present ranges and originate new products.

"This is the division of a company in which the managing director himself is often deeply involved and that is as it should be. It applies particularly if he is an engineer, a technologist or a scientist, but sometimes the closeness of the managing director to R & D can cause conflict between the works managers, the marketing managers and the R & D managers.

"The product managers believe their views should have priority with R & D because they have to cope with the production problems following a new development. The marketing managers feel they should have priority because they have to sell the products; while the managing director is often more concerned with corporate strategy and how new developments will line up with that strategy. It sometimes happens that the managing director takes sides. If he is a marketing man he will tend to see the viewpoint of his marketing managers more clearly. If he is an engineer he will side with his works managers. This is wrong. The managing director must at all times be impartial.

"On some occasions it is not the research and development managers who are at fault, but the marketing managers.

"I read the other day that Prutec, the Prudential venture capital division for high-tech products, have discovered that many of the projects they helped finance have proved harder to sell than anticipated. Of sixty projects only twenty survived and perhaps by now some of those have disappeared.

"It may be that research and development had got it all wrong. It could be that the technologists were over-enthusiastic, or that their marketing strategy was at fault and had not been considered in sufficient depth prior to the launch. To ensure success the first person to be engaged for any new venture must be an outstanding marketing executive. If the chief marketing executive is not a brilliant all-rounder, a multi-disciplined manager, even the best of products may not achieve the success they deserve. So let us blame ourselves before we blame R & D for products which fail. A good product strategy is to ensure in the first place that the marketing is right.

"If they had their way R & D would invest so much in robotics, computer-aided designs, new testing plant and the latest technical magic from Germany, the USA and Japan that the cash flow would be changed dramatically. R & D managers nearly always demand more than they need. There must be tight control on their expenditure or it can get out of hand. The managers can always justify their claims by insisting that the future depends on buying this, or investing in that – it's a form of blackmail by R & D personnel. 'Blackmail' is the wrong word; they are not making demands for their own benefit, but acting in what they consider to be the company's best interests. The threat is used because they, themselves, so enjoy working in the best environment with the best equipment. However, all expenditure by R & D must be costed into the products otherwise it tends to be written off and no one then knows whether the product is really profitable or not.

"Because of the importance of costs, R & D management should attend financial training courses to learn how a negative cash flow, non-profitable orders, the cost of seeking perfection and the cost of time when delays occur affect profits."

Ashton paused and said, "I have to keep switching because there are so many points to be discussed, but I'll be as brief as I can.

"A weakness in some of the multinationals is that R & D management do not know what is taking place in subsidiary companies. In one instance the R & D division of a subsidiary company was working on parallel lines to that of the parent company, developing units away from the standard range and moving into another area of development.

"Now a question: Should a company have a product manager whose objective is solely to seek new products? If so, should he be part of the R & D team?

"My opinion is that such a manager can only be employed by the largest companies to consider the worldwide application of their various products. In the main it should be the marketing executives who seek new ideas and should constantly be on the lookout for new products or new areas to develop.

"Most brainwaves for new developments will come from the managing director or marketing director, but improvements in materials used in production will stem from the R & D division. However, all new materials should undergo exhaustive tests before being introduced into a unit range.

"A main problem with all R & D departments is motivating the technologists, engineers and scientists to keep striving to invent, design and improve products. So many of their brilliant concepts are turned down for one reason or another and that always demotivates. Many a time I have heard an R & D researcher say, 'I don't know why the hell they want this division. They never take any notice of us!'

"There is really only one way to motivate such people and that is to show interest in their work and to give them praise when it is due – and that should be quite often! More managing directors, directors and even managers, whose work is far removed from R & D should still find time to visit this division and to show appreciation of the work. These actions really do motivate.

"Now we turn to the question of investment in R & D. If it is too low, personnel become depressed and results may be poor. If it is too high, too many ideas may emanate from the division, resulting in more products coming out of R & D than can be either manufactured or handled by the sales division. Careful consideration must be given to the investment to get the balance right.

"The next point is that research and development should only vary within narrow limits. Sometimes, however, the managing director himself is the worst offender, continually breaking the rules because he wants to get in on the act. His personal enthusiasm overrides his logical thinking. Let me add quickly that this same enthusiasm can also be aroused in marketing directors, but they have a disadvantage. The managing director is apt to say 'no' to them; but who says 'no' to the managing director?

"Managing directors should be ready to bow to the majority at R & D meetings if the verdict is against their enthusiastic desire to enter a new market. And that, I think, is all – for the time being."

Ashton sat down, amidst applause.

Cathy said, "I must be kinder to our research and development people in the future."

"You did tell me that you have a very good R & D division in your group, Cathy," said Harley.

"We have, but they don't willingly accept outside suggestions. They want the credit for successes while expecting others to take the blame for failures. But now I know the reason. We don't make enough fuss of them and I'll make sure we put that right in the future."

Cathy continued. "I'd like to make a few points:

1. While believing implicitly in R & D, it is sometimes advantageous and less expensive in the long run to buy into new products by acquisition or to manufacture under licence. We took over a company manufacturing mats for entrance halls, offices and factories and this saved endless research and manufacturing problems. We also make under licence a rodent exterminator which put us ahead of our competitors by about a year.
2. Very few managers in any company really study trade magazines published both here and overseas. Someone, preferably a linguist, should do that regularly. It's most rewarding. We developed a fly killer from an advertisement we saw in an Italian magazine and we completely redesigned our vending machines after noticing a beautifully designed unit in a trade magazine published in Canada.
3. Although I agree with all that has been said about brainwaves and the development of new ideas by marketing people, someone has to be severely sceptical about new development. That someone will sometimes be disliked, even hated on occasion, but is necessary to dampen down the early wild excitement and enthusiasms, to demand facts, proof, lists of competitors' satisfied users . . . In any event there must be an adequate screening process. For example: Has it a technical advantage? Will it fill a need? What will the investment be? What additional staff will be required? What extra factory capacity? Will there be any union problems? Can the initial costs be written off within a reasonable time?
4. In spite of what I have just said, crazy ideas must not be ignored – only carefully investigated.
5. At every research and development meeting a list should be made of the ideas and product suggestions. This list should be kept up to date; should be added to, or product ideas deleted.

6. Remember the sixty-four thousand dollar question: 'When a new product is suggested, will it sell?' It may look the best, the quickest, the quietest, the tastiest. But will it sell? Alternatively, what might stop it selling?
7. Value analysis is not heard of so much these days, but it is still applicable. There should be continual analysis of components purchased, the aim being to cut costs by substitution of materials or change to another supplier.
8. My advice to a small company is not to innovate, but follow in the steps of the big boys. Because the small businesses can often act faster and sell better, that product strategy usually works well. There's nothing wrong with a company copying others' ideas, provided patents are not infringed.
9. When considering product strategy remember that buying patterns are always changing.
10. Other factors should be considered when reviewing future product strategy. Will employment rise or fall? The rich, as we know, will always get richer; is that a market to aim for? What regional changes will there be? What taxation changes are likely and what effect will they have? Will educational standards rise? Will social habits change? And, of course, technological and fashion changes are inevitable. If there is a parliamentary election within the next two or three years there are bound to be subsequent changes and these, too, must be considered.

"These points, although discussed during our session on research, also apply to product strategy. It isn't necessary to be a futurologist to have some idea of what might happen in a few years' time. There are books written by experts; they are not always right, but they do provide guidelines. There are government reports, statements by the CBI, British Institute of Management, Institute of

Directors. There are conferences where you can obtain useful information about the future. There are no complete answers, but indications are better than guesswork when considering future company product strategy."

Everyone agreed that Cathy's ten points were worth including in the book. There were further discussions, some good natured banter, and then Ashton said, "There is one aspect of product strategy which is often overlooked, that is design.

"In an R & D division there might not be an original or creative designer. Very few marketing managers are capable of design work allied to feasibility of production. The final design of a product is often an amalgam of the brainchildren of someone in production, in marketing and in R & D. My company has, on several occasions, used the services of the Design Council, which is an offshoot of the Department of Industry. It is government subsidised and in the first design phase there is little cost to a company using the service. In the second phase, if it is reached, the company only meets half the costs. The designers, of course, are all professionals.

"Quick results cannot be expected, but during the last four years or so nearly four thousand companies have used the services of the Design Council. There is now an affiliation between the Design Council and the Building Design Index, to further the needs of design in the building industry.

"We have a lot to learn in the UK about design, but we are fast catching up. My advice to companies is to make use of the facilities offered by the Design Council."

Ashton sat down and after some discussion Harley said, "I think it's about time I had a turn.

"In the advertising world we were continually coming up against the problem of life-cycles. It was either too early to determine the life-cycle, or too late – so why flog a dead horse? How, then, does industry arrive at a life-cycle? Do we wait for sales to fall? Or do we carry on, hoping that one day something better will come along?

"Here are some guidelines which we have used on our clients' behalf in the past.

"First, the life-cycle end is usually determined because people tire of a product. What was once looked upon as a designer's dream is suddenly seen as drab and old-fashioned and sales drop dramatically.

"Second, the product is criticised for lagging behind a competitor's offer. Earlier it was said that a new drive might revive flagging enthusiasm for a product, but that depends to some extent on whether R & D have come up with a replacement. If not, there is no alternative but to continue the life-cycle of that particular product.

"A good case study of product rejuvenation is the Bovril story. Bovril has been a household name for over a hundred years – some life-cycle! Sales began to fall in the early 'eighties by as much as 25 per cent. The famous name was considered to be a little old-fashioned and the product, therefore, must also be old-fashioned.

"Detailed surveys were carried out and a new strategy adopted which included the introduction of star personalities in their advertising campaign. Labels were redesigned, sales promotions increased and sampling tests were carried out throughout the country. Sales rose by some 15 per cent.

"This is a good example because the product had excellent customer acceptance. There was really no need to find a replacement, only to invigorate the marketing campaign. All options must be considered before an end to a life-cycle.

"Sometimes companies make an each-way bet. A new product arrives which is very similar to the old one but has one or two improvements. There is a sales drive for the new product, but the old one is not replaced in case it is occasionally still required. It's often far better to drop the old product when a new one is introduced.

"Usually it is obvious when a life-cycle is ending, except to those who refuse to accept the truth. This could include the managing director himself. The product has been identified with his company for many years and he can't bear the thought of discarding it. Or it could be the brainchild of an R & D wizard, or a marketing enthusiast, or any other manager – they will not admit that anything they developed could possibly become out of date.

"Do we marketing people agree on a life-cycle when it is launched? Will it sell for three years, five years, ten years?

"If a five-year plan is laid down for a new product there is a clear objective to find a replacement before that time elapses. This policy is essential if the product comes under the heading of a fad: skate boards, yo-yos and, more recently, computer games. The way to make big profits out of fads is to determine a short life-cycle, reap the rewards quickly and then get out. Let the latecomers lose their money.

"Apart from fads there are usually three stages of a life-cycle. First, the burst of initial enthusiasm, then a plateau when sales even out and, finally, the slide. That is the time to get out.

"When the slide starts it's a good idea to find out if the product can be put to other uses before it is discarded. The person who discovers new uses for old products is worthy of high rewards. Many years ago Kleenex ran a campaign inviting suggestions from their customers for the use of tissues and suggestions poured in. Many of them were used in advertising.

"Finally, a life-cycle can be a great danger to one-product companies. There comes a time when patents dry up and competitors enter the field. Polaroid is a good example of what happens when this occurs."

Harley paused as the door opened and a trolley was

wheeled in laden with coffee and biscuits. He announced a ten-minute break, left the room and made for his bedroom. As he opened the door he heard the telephone bell ringing. It was Cathy.

"I tried to catch up with you, but you were racing along. Mike, what's happening? What happened when you were in London? I was thinking of you most of the night."

"I'll tell you in a day or so."

"Why not now?"

"Because I could be on a wild goose chase. Don't worry, Cathy. You'll be the first to know."

When she rang off he asked the operator for a London number. Five minutes later he decided that he certainly was not on a wild goose chase.

When the session recommenced Harley said, "I'll continue, but not where I left off. I shall copy Cathy and give you a few more things to bear in mind.

1. What should we take into account when considering a new product? Can it be sold by the present sales force? Will the sales force have to be increased? Do we need new salesmen, well versed in a special technology? What will the additional sales costs be?
2. Can it compete? This is a question which is too often answered by those emotionally involved. They wave aside all doubts and problems, including the possible actions of competitors. As mentioned earlier, someone not so involved should ask questions and insist on getting true answers. This point is worth repeating because it is so often overlooked.
3. Decide on plans for quality testing of new products to avoid teething troubles.
4. Having got the costings right, the next question is will the price we set leave sufficient margin for

distributors, commissions, royalties etc.? We'll discuss this question under pricing strategy, but it does come under product strategy as well.
5. Can the product be patented in whole or part?
6. What share of the market are we aiming for? This question can be allied to segmentation by customer, area etc.
7. Have we the staff to cope with the demand?
8. How will competitors react?
9. Are we quite sure that the present product cannot be modified or altered to save the costs of starting a new unit from scratch?
10. Will the effort be worth the headaches?"

Drake said, "There are always problem headaches, but clear thinking, good leadership and objective decision-making can get us off the aspirin trail." Turning to Harley he said, "Mike, you're producing books. What is your product strategy?"

Harley answered, "I'm still learning, but there is our back list, mostly non-fiction, and we weed out books from that list every time a reprint is due. If the demand remains reasonable we reprint, otherwise we look out for a new book on the same subject.

"We receive dozens of unsolicited manuscripts every month and turn down 99.5 per cent of them, but our product strategy is to read every one and hope that a winner will turn up one day. Most of all, we rely on our editors to seek out books worth publishing and suggest ideas to authors for them to develop into books – something similar to what we are now doing. And what we are now achieving is the forerunner of a stream of bestsellers. We can cover every subject, from sport to computer usage.

"We're very lucky, we have three authors whose books sell in millions. They're a fine cushion against those many books we publish that turn out to be unprofitable.

"Now you know my personal product strategy for the future."

Cathy said, "But you're emotionally involved."

"Sure! But I'm one of those marketing people we talked about – I can smell a winner a mile off! But that's enough about books. What next?"

Ashton took an envelope from his pocket and extracted from it a printed page. He said, "This is an article printed in the *Heating and Air Conditioning* journal. I'd like to read the first few paragraphs. It's headed 'Nu-look for the fan convector'.

> Not being able to see the wood for the trees is something which we have all probably experienced at least once, but one would not expect a whole industry to be struck by it. Nevertheless, onto the fan convector market now comes a product with such a different and yet simple design one is forced to wonder why, in over 30 years of fan convector manufacturing, it has not been seen before. And this development comes not from an existing heating manufacturer, but from a fan manufacturer, Nu-Aire Ltd.
>
> This is less strange when one knows that the main feature of the new model, its slimness (hence the name Slimheat) is obtained because of a change in fan/motor placement from that previously used. But from this one central idea Nu-Aire then proceeded to rethink virtually every facet of the standard fan convector and even brought in an industrial designer with no preconceived idea of what a fan convector even looked like. Hence the unusual look of the final product . . .

Ashton crumpled up the cutting and said, "There's no point in my reading on – the rest wouldn't interest you. What struck me is that there must be many opportunities in manufacturing for rethinking a product from scratch –

a total new concept. That, surely, must be good product strategy."

Harley nodded. "You're right, Ian. I've played tennis since I was a child and I'd like to discuss tennis racquets. Up till the mid-seventies we used racquets with frames made of wood laminate. Dunlop and Slazengers had a virtual monopoly in that field. Then someone had a rethink and a new idea was developed – the graphite frame. This was followed by frames made of mixtures of graphite and fibreglass; then new shapes and special hotspots. This new rethink market has been captured by Taiwan manufacturers and also ski manufacturers, who are able to apply their technological skills to tennis racquet frames. A virtual monopoly was lost because competition had a rethink and developed a new product strategy for tennis racquets."

Cathy asked, "Have you got a metal racquet?"

"Not yet, but if the book is a great success I shall be able to afford one."

There followed a short, sparkling interlude with everyone giving their examples of rethinking. After a while Harley said, "How about concluding with a few more examples of product strategy? Who'll make a start?"

Cathy stood up and said, "No-one has mentioned the product mix – such a favourite term with marketing people. They love mixes: the marketing mix, the product mix . . . All it means is making certain that all products interlock and one doesn't stand out like a sore thumb.

"My final point is you should ensure that all suppliers of component parts are reliable. Manufacturers are let down time and time again by suppliers who maybe have quoted the cheapest prices, but also give the worst service."

Harley then added some thoughts of his own.

"First, to sustain growth it is no longer possible to be

insular. We must export and when a new product is suggested we should ask a most pertinent quesion: Will there be an overseas market for it?

"Second, there must be a continual evaluation of the complete product range with no sacred cows. Bad sellers must go! And that's all from me. Over to you, Colin."

Drake said, "I've nothing really new to offer. We've covered most of the ground, but we haven't considered the buyers' viewpoint on product development. In my case it's the retail buyer, but the principles are the same. During a lunchtime meeting one of our biggest buyers said: 'Manufacturers still don't give enough consideration to the changing needs of their customers; suppliers take too long to adapt. Product quality is being lowered so that prices may be more competitive. This lowering of quality only loses business in the long run. Also, it leads to own-label products taking over. Sometimes it seems that too much emphasis is placed on consumer testing and not enough on the advice of a retailer as to which products will sell and which will remain on the shelves. Too many claims are made – exaggerated claims – for products which cannot be substantiated.'

"These are not his exact words, but they cover his viewpoint."

Harley thanked Colin and then Ashton said, "I'd like to make a suggestion before we break.

"The next session is on pricing strategy. Bruce mentioned earlier that it might be preferable to change the sessions and discuss advertising strategy, before product and pricing. I objected and we all agreed on the great importance of both product and pricing strategies.

"Now I want to make a plea to accept Bruce's suggestion and devote our time to advertising this afternoon and leave pricing until tomorrow."

Bruce said, "A convert so quickly!"

Ashton answered, "Not at all, but I thought I could save time. Let me explain. When I left school I was articled to an accountant and I qualified before I was twenty-two. It was easier in those days. After a year or so of auditing I decided that accountancy was not for me. In fact I had been persuaded to take it up by my parents. I'd always wanted to be an engineer, so I decided to become one. Eventually I went to Leeds University and got my BSc in engineering.

"The rest of the story you know. I was first in production and then in sales as a sales engineer, then export and finally marketing. I'm not giving you my life story to blow my own trumpet, but to explain my reason for suggesting that we switch sessions. Pricing is a subject which I really understand from every angle – accountancy, production, marketing and top management. I've lectured on pricing and written articles on the subject.

"I'm willing to write a précis this evening. I have my notes with me and I can easily get them duplicated by the office here and you'll have the précis early tomorrow morning. We can have a discussion at the usual starting time, 9 a.m., and add points to my memo. What do you think of that, Mike?"

"A marvellous idea, Ian. I'm all for it." And so were the others, who expressed their appreciation of Ashton's willingness to work overtime.

Ashton added, "In any event, the advertising session will be covered mainly by you, Mike. You know more than any of us on the subject and I'm sure you'll need some extra time."

12 A Conflict of Views

It was another hot day and lunch was served on the terrace. Harley had a slice of cold beef and a green salad, but as he was anxious to make more telephone calls he cut out the sweet and coffee.

He had been sharing the table with Colin Drake and Bruce Hayes. After he left Bruce said, "He's either a workaholic or needs to attend a course on time management. I make it a rule that no one telephones me when I'm away and I don't telephone the office unless I require some urgent information. What's the use of delegating, if you're always on someone's tail?"

Drake agreed, but added, "In the world of advertising everyone telephones everyone else all the time – it's a sign of dynamism, or something. Mike's still living in the past. He hasn't yet caught up with the fact that he is now in the most slow-moving of businesses. Try asking a bookseller to obtain a book quickly for you. The answer is always: 'I can't because.' Then come the excuses: 'It was only published last week and we haven't received our copies yet'; 'The rep said there's been some trouble with the binding'; 'They never hurry with special orders'; 'They've had a warehouse problem'. Dear Mike wants to change all that, but I wonder if he can."

Cathy, sitting with Ian Ashton, only had a prawn salad and coffee. When she saw Harley leaving the terrace she pretended not to notice but a few minutes later, telling

Ian that she had some letters to write, she followed in Harley's footsteps.

Cathy was soon knocking on Mike's door. He was on the telephone and she heard him say, "OK. I'm coming to town tomorrow and we'll get things settled. I'll be away from here by about four o'clock I should think. See you." And he replaced the receiver.

Turning he said, "Cathy, I'd love to have you in my bedroom, but not now."

"Mike, what's the matter with you? You're phoning London all the time. What's happening?"

"I told you during the coffee break."

"You told me nothing. Why? Don't you trust me?"

"Of course I do, Cathy, but you may give me the right advice, which I don't want to hear, or the wrong advice which will only upset you if I brush it aside."

"That's typical of you, Mike. First you take me into your confidence and then you clam up. That was the trouble when we were together. You're always being so beastly chauvinistic. But I think I know what you're up to."

"Do you? There's a clever girl. Tell me."

"You're going to buy out Corbett's for a £100 million in Harley shares, plus £10 cash."

"Ha ha, very funny! Cathy, I've some calls to make."

"You want me to go?"

"That's right!"

"You don't change, do you?"

"Who does?"

"Shall I tell you what you are really planning?"

"Yes," said Harley, laughing. "What am I planning to do?"

"You're selling out to another publisher who won't need your staff. It's the obvious solution, isn't it? Harley's business can continue, if they allow it to do so, which I'm sure they will, and you get the cash. Am I right?"

"No. As those who are lying in their teeth but don't want to be proved liars and those who daren't let the truth be known always say, no comment!"

"That means I'm right!"

"If you say so."

She sat down on the bed next to him and held his hand. "Mike, I'm still very fond of you and I do want to help you."

"Fine! Then marry me."

"What?"

"Marry me."

"Just like that?"

"Yes, just like that!"

"What a romantic man you are, Mike."

He turned and looked straight at her. "But what's your answer, Cathy?"

"No. What did you expect?"

Mike said, "I thought that would be your answer. But don't you ever forgive and forget?"

"Yes, often. I can forgive, but I can't forget that you left me and then married another woman." Then, after a pause, "But I still want to help you, Mike."

He kissed her. They remained silent for a few minutes, then she stood up, patted his head, waved a hand and left the room.

Harley felt a little sad, but he stayed resolute. If you want to keep a secret, don't tell anyone – not your best friend, your nearest and dearest, your partner, no one. Even the most honest, decent person can, inadvertently, pass on a secret by saying, "I know you won't say anything but . . ." Just keep it to yourself. That was his dictum.

He sighed, muttering to himself, "Maybe I am a chauvinist pig."

13 Advertising

Harley had a faculty common to many leaders in industry. At night he could switch off his mind and fall asleep within seconds; similarly during the day he could forget a problem and concentrate on the work in hand. Without this ability to switch off, few executives could cope and lack of this faculty is sometimes the reason why those in middle-management fail to reach a higher plateau. Harley believed that problems were there to be solved, not worried about, and problem-solving was only an exercise in clear thinking, while worry or fear of failure took its toll in stress illnesses.

Harley's mind was concentrating on advertising when he opened the afternoon session. "Let me begin," he said, "by asking a question: Can any of you recollect an advertisement, or a series of advertisements or TV commercials which you disliked, found distasteful, or wondered how any creative person could have produced such rubbish?"

Cathy immediately answered, "All those wretched detergent advertisements with simpering women showing astonishment that brand *X* could be so much better than brand *Y*."

"And you consider that poor advertising?"

"They certainly don't appeal to me!"

"Well, Cathy, the fact is that type of test advertising is a winner. Because you have an analytical and critical mind you mustn't endow others with your powers of perception. It's how the majority react to an advertising campaign that matters; minorities can't always be catered for.

"Although these advertisements may not appeal to you, they work."

Ashton said, "There's one advertising campaign that makes me feel slightly sick. It's for a Japanese car, a hatchback, and it depicts a man's head from which protrudes a growth, supposedly to convey the impression of intensive thinking. Alongside there are comparisons between their hatchbacks and competitive cars. I find that advertisement most distasteful. Surely a growth on the head can only have ugly connotations and would make many readers turn over the page quickly. What justification can there be for that advertisement? Where is the appeal?"

Harley said, "I can't tell you. I feel the same way about it. Someone liked it obviously and we must remember that no creative artist, no advertising consortium of decision-makers or presenters of a campaign can ever see anything wrong with what they have produced. All the agencies with which I have been associated indulged in self-criticism, until the plan was finalised. Then all, or at least most, of us believed that it was 100 per cent perfect, original and the best of its kind.

"We had to think that way, didn't we? The strange part is that we were always criticising the work of other agencies. We'd probably have knocked hell out of the advertisement you just mentioned, Ian, but if we'd come up with the same idea, would we have been so self-critical? We rarely took much notice either of our clients' objections.

"If the client should have the temerity to suggest a change the admen will pretend to go along with him. They will use such sentences as, 'I see your point, D.J.' 'That's a contemplative slant, B.Y.' 'Good!' 'I think that's what we're aiming for. Thank you, S.P.'

"That's standard lip service, but very little is going to change. To most admen only their own creative people are right. Those who criticise don't understand advertising."

"You sound like a poacher turned gamekeeper," said Ashton.

"Not at all! I'm telling you the facts. That's why marketing managers should learn more about advertising, so that they can criticise from strength."

"Are there any other advertisement dislikes?"

"My pet hate," said Drake, "was a series of TV commercials for British Airways. They depicted a floating city, New York, advancing slowly from the horizon to cover the sky over an avenue of suburban houses.

"The effect of that commercial on some people was frightening, picturing as it did a floating city shrouded in a mystical glow, apparently blown across the Atlantic by some unknown force.

"And that commercial was supposed to motivate people to fly BA. There was not one real benefit in it for potential users of the airline."

Harley agreed. "Yes, it didn't appeal to me. But how do we find winners?"

"You tell us!" said Bruce Hayes.

"I will, but first, are there any more dislikes? How about you, Bruce?"

Hayes said, "I object to faces in advertisements – the face of the chairman, managing director, author, tycoon . . . But chairmen like seeing themselves in print, especially if they are hoping to appeal to city investors. And authors apparently delight in seeing their faces on book jackets.

"Neither does much harm, but I think we all quickly tire of the faces of tycoons especially if we see them almost daily. My pet dislike was the series depicting two tycoons on the takeover trail. One looked a little like a con man and the other a salesman for secondhand cars.

I'm sure their wives thought them most handsome, their children thought them glamorous, their associates looked upon them as fine men. No doubt they were, but that didn't come over in the photographs which to my mind created an entirely different impression.

"I can understand the use of film stars or sports stars, but why tycoons? What's a tycoon's face got to do with his ability to improve someone else's business?"

Harley shrugged his shoulders. "It works sometimes but, I agree, generally it's a loser. When I was in advertising I never played up to the client by suggesting that we use his picture, although from the point of view of salesmanship it can often be a clincher. The client would exclaim, 'No one wants to see my face, do they?' followed very quickly by, 'Have you got a good photographer?'

"Well, we've made the point that even the best creative people slip up occasionally and it's difficult for them to accept criticism from outsiders. That's why I'm emphasising that marketing managers must speak from knowledge and the strength that knowledge gives them. We marketing people must not give way if we think the admen are wrong.

"Now let's get back to basics. It's safe to assume that most display advertising and TV commercials will be placed through agents, but marketing directors must realise that creative thinkers often know little about salesmanship or marketing generally. Yet advertising is only selling under a different guise.

"Most advertisements are designed to persuade us to do something which we have not, perhaps, previously contemplated: to switch to another make of car, to enjoy a cruise instead of sunbathing at the seaside, to take up a timeshare offer, to buy fridge *X* instead of fridge *Y*. In the trade press, technically sophisticated products are advertised for the sole purpose of influencing the minds of purchasing authorities or decision makers.

"An advertisement is a persuader, a mind changer, and that is exactly the aim of the salesmen. If Mrs Brown is already using brand *X* no persuasion is needed. The ad. is only a reminder to her of how good that brand is. The object of the advertisement is to persuade thousands of housewives using brand *Y* to switch to brand *X*. That is salesmanship, so let us remember when we are planning an advertising campaign that we are only employing salesmanship in print or on TV.

"In salesmanship there are several steps to the order. The first step recognised by all salesmen is to attract and hold attention, to be followed by the creation of interest. These steps are often overlooked by creative admen. They may design a good and attractive attention-getter but they miss out on the second step, the essential one of maintaining interest. The reader, or the viewer, has his attention attracted and is then let down by the subsequent film or copy.

"Here is an example. A salesman is selling advertising signs to shopkeepers. He calls on a shop owner, Mr Brown, and begins, 'Good morning Mr Brown'. Then, before Mr Brown can return the greeting, the salesman throws a handful of coins on to the floor. The surprised shopkeeper wonders if it is a promotion gift, but the salesman continues, 'You are throwing away money every hour of every day, because people are passing by your windows instead of stopping. You want them to stop and our advertising signs will achieve that for you . . .'

"What is happening? The salesman commands immediate attention, but that is followed by the big letdown. The shopkeeper feels annoyed and disappointed and will probably quickly show him the door with 'Not today, thank you'.

"That approach was actually once taught to salesmen

of vending machines. The salesman made the first step by attracting immediate attention, but that was not enough. After the attention-getter there must immediately be a worthwhile benefit to hold the interest of the buyer.

"The same principles apply to advertising, TV and radio commercials.

"Do any of you remember an advertisement for a Siemens washing machine, a double-page spread? On the righthand side was depicted the machine top, on which stood a tall red pencil. The caption read: Try this on any other washing machine at 1,000 rpm and see how well it stands up.

"Now that attracted attention. The copy maintained interest by explaining that although there was nothing revolutionary about 1,000 rpm, there was about a non-vibrating 1,000 rpm machine which resulted in clothes with fewer creases, less crumpled and dry as any other machine on the market.

"That was good follow-up copy. There are some wonderfully creative people about. It's just a question of finding them.

"To recap. An advertisement must attract immediate attention to the product or service – not to a personality nor, for that matter, a beautiful blonde with few clothes on. Then benefits must follow.

"Cinzano Bianco used the personality cult in a series of TV commercials which most of us thought highly successful. They depicted the late Leonard Rossiter and Joan Collins in different situations; but whatever the situation, invariably, the ending showed Leonard accidentally pouring the wine over Joan Collins' gown.

"However, the Cinzano company decided to cancel the campaign because although people laughed at the antics of Joan and Leonard they forgot the purpose of the advertisement, which was to sell Cinzano Bianco."

Hayes said, "That change of mind surprised me, but

now I can see the Cinzano viewpoint. How about pretty girls? Their inclusion can't be bad advertising, surely!"

"The same rule applies," said Harley. "The prettier the girl the more attention is directed towards her; the less clothes she is wearing the more she will be studied. The risk is that we men only remember the beautiful smiling young girls leaning against the product, looking at the product, patting the product, lying alongside the product . . . rather than the product itself."

"But," said Cathy, "it meets with your criterion of attracting attention."

"Yes, Cathy, but there is no real link with the product – that's the weakness. The admen are pandering to their clients' weaknesses. When they suggest to the client that it would be a good idea to have a glamour girl in the ad. that client won't demur for long; more than likely he'll insist on being present at the photographic sessions. It's a line most clients fall for, to use a cliché, hook, line and sinker.

"The exceptions to the 'girlie' rule, of course, are advertisements for perfumes, deodorants, showers and suchlike.

"The point I want to emphasise," continued Harley, "is that *the attention must be on the product* and there must be no immediate switch from the attention-getter to the product or copy.

"After our attention has been attracted and we have been persuaded to read the copy and study the product, so that we learn all about the benefits, there must be some motivator to encourage a reasonable proportion of readers or viewers to act. In selling this is referred to as 'the close'. The sole criterion is: Will it sell the product?

"Finally, all marketing men should beware of 'so what?' advertisements – TV commercials in which actors or actresses speak or sing in a language sounding something like garbled Chinese, Japanese or Russian. Only the script man really knows what it's all about. The advertisements are so clever that, not understanding their objective, our reaction is 'So what?' 'So what?' advertisements and commercials are always failures."

Harley stopped to drink some water and Hayes said, "I presume you are now going to tell us how to choose an agency."

Harley replaced the glass on the table and said, "No, not yet. Don't be so impatient! First we must consider some of the wider implications of advertising and the best way to do that and to maintain reader interest is for each of us to contribute a number of advertising factors."

Cathy began. "Here is some advice for the small-scale advertiser: Don't be misled by the mock-up of an advertisement which is usually very well sketched, wash-painted or photographed. Unfortunately the subsequent advertisement in the newspaper often doesn't look nearly so attractive as the mock-up. The facial features are hardly distinguishable, the print is not too clear and that most perfect of products of which the client is so proud looks very ordinary. Advertisers should allow for the artist's endeavours to make his work appealing, so that a four-inch double column has all the appearance of a half-page advertisement. Usually the fault is trying to please a client by cramming too much into a small space.

"My second point I learned by hard experience. Designers too often design to please themselves and not the customers.

"The third point is never advertise a product before adequate stocks are available to satisfy the demand. This mistake occurs regularly even with the largest companies and it is always the result of bad management and bad planning. Isn't that right, Colin?"

Drake agreed. "Most certainly! In the consumer field customers are infuriated by having to go from shop to shop seeking an advertised product, because supplies have not yet been delivered or the retailer has run out of stock and has not yet been able to replenish it."

Bruce Hayes said, "My wife regularly finds that dresses advertised are not available even at listed stockists. Suppliers are often unhelpful and don't know which shop might be stocking the dress and they never offer to find out and telephone back. That's an example of bad marketing, isn't it?"

Drake came in again. "Cathy, you're right. We marketing people are to blame for the almost unforgiveable mistake of spending money on advertising without first ensuring that supplies are available in the shops." He paused, glanced at a note he had made, then said, "Now for my point: The managing director of a small to medium-sized business should never attempt to compete with the big advertisers. That way lies bankruptcy!

"What usually happens is this. The managing director is told by his marketing director, who in turn has been told by his salesmen, that retailers insist on having details of advertising campaigns before placing orders and that the salesmen are being turned down because of lack of advertising. What is overlooked is that the plea for increased expenditure on advertising is often the salesman's excuse for not succeeding.

"What is the managing director to do? Increase advertising and make losses, or train his salesmen to be more proficient in their work?

"Even on the shelves in supermarkets you will find unadvertised goods: bread, biscuits, drinks and many other items. They are there because they are very good quality products or highly competitive. When such unadvertised products fail to sell it means that there has been little repeat business which, in turn, may mean failure of quality, packaging, or living up to the claims made on the packets. Obviously the big demand will always be for the heavily advertised products, but that doesn't mean the smaller manufacturers can't get their share of the market without such advertising."

Ashton agreed. "Yes, Colin, but there is a snag when products are sold through distributors. Their salesmen are sometimes woefully weak, in fact just order-takers. Distributors should therefore be backed by advertising to motivate their salesmen, but what does the managing director of the smaller company do about that?"

Cathy said, "Please let me answer that one. We used distributors for some time and we backed them with only modest advertising; but we found that training was the answer.

"Salesmen selling to distributors must be outstandingly good and they, in their turn, should motivate, train and assist the distributors' salesmen to achieve success."

"Should that advice go into the book?" asked Bruce Hayes. "After all, we are supposed to be helping marketing people to plan their advertising campaign."

Harley answered immediately, "But we must tell the truth – when to advertise as well as when not to advertise – yes, it will go in. Next please!" Harley smiled apologetically. "Sorry, Bruce, that was a bit curt. I didn't intend it to be, but we must show warts and all, don't you agree?"

Hayes nodded. "I'm not upset," he said, "don't worry."

Cathy interrupted, "May I return to ladies' wear? Why does that trade advertise summerwear in the spring and winterwear while summer is still with us? Why don't they advertise heavily during the actual seasons? In the summer we buy our summer dresses and in the winter we buy our winter dresses. We're not such good planners-ahead, you know. And another point: Why do ladies' wear manufacturers use such identikit, witless looking, insipid models? We certainly can't identify with them . . ."

Cathy continued her diatribe against the ladies' wear

manufacturers' advertising campaigns and Harley let her carry on for a while.

Then he said, "Let's switch to another subject now: How do we judge an advertising campaign? How do we know if it has been worth while? A question I used to be asked most frequently was: How do I check on results? – a question almost impossible to answer even when advertisements have been couponed."

Ashton interrupted, "But returned coupons do give a definite indication surely of the effectiveness of the advertisement?"

Harley answered, "Yes, but they don't indicate whether a more appealing advertisement wouldn't have brought in even better results."

"That's carping!" said Ashton.

Harley smiled. "Maybe, Ian, but that was an argument I've used to have an account transferred from a competitive agency to my own. Yes, of course coupons do give some indication. Also, when brand *X* is given an advertising plug for a month or so with heavy expenditure there can be a check on results if there is an upsurge in sales. But when brand *X* is advertised all the year round it is difficult to assess results.

"There are so many factors to be considered. A series of strikes could affect the best of campaigns, a very hot summer, a very cold winter, or unseasonable weather conditions – an economic crisis . . . Unfortunately we cannot always predict in advance. There is little point in assessing returns from normal advertising campaigns. The exceptions are those with special offers. Advertising should be a marketing cost, a percentage of sales or profits; or by product assessment, which can vary from product to product. Once the expenditure has been fixed it should be forgotten, provided there have been forecasts. If sales are up to forecasts, or costs are down on forecasts, whatever the expenditure on advertising it must have been worthwhile. It will have contributed to the success of the company. If, however, the forecasts aren't met there may have to be a revision. My advice is always to allocate – and forget.

"Of course, spectacularly original, effective advertising campaigns can result in an upsurge in sales even during a depression. But we're back again now to basics. It all depends on the advertising agent and his creative staff.

"Going back even further, it all depends on the marketing director and his ability to choose the right advertising agency for his company."

Cathy said, "That's all very well, but we may not pick the best of advertising agents; we may not be able to choose the greatest of creative teams. Then we have to make do with our decision. How do we mitigate failure, or make even more certain of some success? Surely one way would be to ensure that our advertising is targeted correctly. Mike, you know more about that than any of us and these are facts that should go into the book."

"You're right, Cathy, and the marketing director must be aware of the surveys available to assist in targeting.

"There is the National Readership Survey of some 30,000 people which identifies occupation, status, incomes, house ownership, reading habits, etc.

"There is the Businessman's Survey. Their sample is about 3,000, but again they give data to assist in targeting ads directed towards the businessman.

"There is the Target Index itself, which is based on about 26,000 people and gives a breakdown of brands and services.

"There is BARB, the British Audience Research Bureau; and ACORN, A Classification of Residential Neighbourhoods, to provide information about housing groups – types, sizes, gardens etc. And, of course, there are the data provided by all newspapers and magazines.

"All we can do, Cathy, is to include in the book advice

on where the information can be obtained. Is that good enough?"

"I suppose so," she replied.

"Right! Then let's move on towards fragmentation and selectivity. Mass messages are essential for some products, while for others selectivity is the answer. That is why there is such a boom in advertising in giveaway glossy magazines for the top end of the market and free newspapers for the targeting of suburban householders. There are also specific magazines concerned with country life, good living, furniture . . . All have specialist appeal. This advertising fragmentation should be carefully considered by marketing managers and especially by PR personnel.

"Regional newspapers also have a definite part to play in targeting for specific areas and classes of buyers. It's up to the marketing manager to obtain all this information before listening to the adman's proposals."

There followed a brief discussion after which Harley asked, "Are there any more points of view before we tackle the difficult subject of choosing an agency?"

Ashton said, "I should like to elaborate on industrial advertising where the general level is between bad and mediocre. Photographs rarely highlight the excellent features of a product; the layouts are seemingly designed by an engineering draughtsman rather than a creative artist, and the copy written by a handyman on one of his off days."

"Hold on," interrupted Harley, "that's a wide-ranging statement! I've seen some very good advertisements in trade and technical publications."

"I would like to finish," said Ashton.

"Sorry! Only I used to feel that my agency was pretty good at industrial advertising."

"I'm sure you were. But remember I used the word

'general'. There are a few exceptions where well designed advertisements are produced. Unfortunately they're all too few, I'm sure you'll agree with that, Mike. Later you'll advise us on how to choose an agency that could provide a good service for the industrial advertiser."

Harley shrugged his shoulders. "OK, Ian, carry on."

"I'll continue," went on Ashton, "by emphasising that I am referring to the 80 per cent of industrial advertisements which depict a drawing or photograph of a product; a boring list of features taken from the instruction manual with most unoriginal captions. You know the kind of thing: 'The best turret on the market' or 'The very best machine tool' or even 'It's our best ever!'

"Very rarely does the caption meet your maxim, Mike, of attracting attention. Anyway the copy is usually only read by competitors and is skipped by buyers.

"I know this is strong criticism, but pick up any technical or trade journal and you'll find that the editorial copy and the articles are good, but not the advertisements. Possibly that's because too many chief executives believe all they have to do is to show a product and it will sell itself. That doesn't happen. I suggest that all marketing directors in the industrial field pay as much attention to the layout of their advertisements and copy as do the marketing executives in the consumer field.

"So who is to blame for this dull advertising? First the agencies who, because there is little profit in industrial advertising, are not deeply interested. They'll fight and fight again for £1 million a year expenditure, but not when all that is being spent is, perhaps, £20,000 in a year. The effort required to design an appealing series of advertisements for *The Plumbers' Gazette* or *The Gasket Manufacturers' Magazine* arouses little enthusiasm.

"From the agency's viewpoint, and this I know for a fact, they are not interested because they tend to believe that the client is not really interested either. A sales manager is probably just told 'Put in a few ads and see if they work'! There is even sometimes a belief on the part of the client that no one really takes any interest in advertisements in industrial or technical publications.

"This, of course, is wrong. Interest is lacking because the advertisements are not appealing. This industrial advertising lethargy should end. Agencies should wake up to the very great field of industrial advertising, which could grow and grow if they provided the right services. Clients should demand quality in their advertisements, as they should demand quality in their products, and every ad. should stress buyer benefits.

"Just in case you think I'm too biased, let me tell you about a very good advertisement which shows what can be done. It was created for the manufacturers of toughened glass. The objective was to show how the glass would withstand almost any stress. The advertisement showed one glass, repeated four times. In the glass was a watch drowned in hydrochloric acid, an immediate attention-getter. The watch was shown disintegrating a little in photograph two, a lot more disintegrated in photograph three and almost disappearing in photograph four. The captions and the copy were hardly necessary; the benefits were there to see. The acid had destroyed the watch, but the glass was unharmed. Anyone in the market for toughened glass would certainly be most intrigued."

Harley said, "The problem is that the cost of space in most technical and trade publications is not high and if an agency is working on a 15 per cent commission fee they don't make much out of these assignments."

Drake added, "Another aspect is that in the consumer field the advertiser has a mass of readership information so the advertisements can be clearly targeted to the right audiences. I understand that it's rare for similar data to be available for the trade and technical press."

He had hardly stopped speaking before Cathy said, "May I say my piece? When we were selling our industrial products direct our agency advised us on marketing, exhibitions, direct mail, public relations . . . We paid a set fee and the agency therefore didn't have to rely solely on the commission element."

Harley said, "Cathy, I think you're referring to a time when your company was smaller than it is today. You probably didn't have the expertise to advise on exhibitions, direct mail etc. But the modern marketing manager, certainly the marketing director, ought to know all about these subjects and shouldn't need any help from an agency. However, I do agree that in the smaller companies such an agency can be of great assistance."

Ashton continued. "My final point is that whatever we spend on advertising must be well spent. There should not be such a low creative profile in the industrial advertising field. That's all."

Harley looked at his watch. "There's time to finish this session before tea and then afterwards we can cover promotions.

"Before we discuss finding the right agency I want to clarify a couple of points. If an adman read the chapter in our book based on this session he would criticise us for not making clear the impact of indirect benefits.

"Here is an example: When, in a TV commercial, a macho action man plugs an underarm deodorant the indirect benefit is that being macho means playing to win, driving fast without fear of body odour. Male viewers are supposed to identify with that macho image and queue up for the underarm deodorant.

"And another example: There are no real benefits driven home in the excellent series of Heineken beer advertisements. There is no mention of high quality ingredients or that the beer awakens our taste buds. What it does stress is that the beer reaches the parts other beers don't reach. What, then, is the important indirect benefit? Simple! We'll all feel much better for drinking Heineken.

"That series of advertisements is well rivalled by Courage's commercials which show confirmed Courage drinkers finding many different reasons for escaping to the pub, to be followed by the great joy of drinking the beer, the indirect benefits being that Courage beer brings pleasure, joy and happiness.

"I had to make that point clear about indirect benefits, otherwise we should be criticised for not understanding the purpose of creative thinking.

"Now, aside from industrial advertising which we have all agreed should be improved, we want to know why in more general advertising some ads or commercials are so brilliant while others make us wonder and ask ourselves the question I mentioned earlier – what was that all about? The problem is not so much finding the right agency as getting the right personnel in that agency.

"Let us consider life, generally. Any twenty doctors will have had much the same form of training, yet at least two will probably be, if not uncaring, not exactly caring either, or deeply concerned about their patients. Sixteen will probably be hard working, not brilliant GP's but good, average doctors doing their very best. And two will be outstanding; fine diagnosticians, good psychologists, really caring for their patients.

"The same applies in a different context to golfers, cricketers, footballers. Top golfers earn a fortune because they are so brilliant, but the others teach at their golf clubs for a living and never make the grade on the circuits.

"It's the same with managers, or artists, or the creative admen. Cathy, I must apologise. When I say admen it is, of course, a generic term for everyone in advertising. Some of the most brilliant creative artists, some of the finest thinkers, are women."

"Thank you," said Cathy. "I was beginning to wonder

when you were going to say something like that."

"The top men and women are really brilliant and the results show in outstanding campaigns. But what happens if your account is handled by a team from the second or third eleven? Remember, you'll be charged the same fee, whoever is assigned to your account.

"The answer is first to check the company carefully, but a lot more about that later. Sometimes the smaller agencies can produce better results for the smaller advertisers. It is most important to be really critical when a presentation is made or an idea put forward. Don't be hoodwinked or misled by excellent self-praise video films, exceptional sketches or such remarks as, 'We might go for *A*, he's good!' or '*B* will be great.' – both well-known personalities.

"Bandying names about is standard practice for admen. My advice, therefore, is to be bloody-minded. Don't agree with anything unless you are sure that the commercial will sell your products.

"Finally, admen really enjoy spending their clients' money. Overseas locations make the toughest of them misty-eyed. Others love providing a lot of unnecessary action, all very costly but giving great pleasure to those directing the scenes. Most ad. producers are frustrated film directors; but stars are only worth using if they really help to sell the product, not just themselves. All clear?"

Drake said, "From now on I'm going to be a most difficult buyer, even if our agency waves goodbye to us."

Harley said, "You needn't worry about that! If an agency wants out you can be quite sure that within months one or two of their top executives will be leaving to start on their own, so go with them. It happens all the time.

"It's a good idea, especially for smaller businesses, to use such new organisations. The ex-executives from the giants will give their all to begin with then eventually they too will have their second and third elevens on which I'll elaborate later. In the meantime, Colin, I'd like you to continue on the theme of finding the right agency, before I make my comments.

"Foster Biscuits are very large advertisers and any of the giant agencies would fight hard for your account. You have changed your agency three times in the last seven years, Colin. Why? Naturally, you can only give a generalised answer. We wouldn't expect a specific comment on the various agencies you've used."

Drake said, "The answer is quite simple. There is little to choose between the dozen or so leading advertising agencies, they will all meet any criteria set. They employ highly creative people; they have their marketing research divisions; they don't have to employ outside media buyers; they have the muscle to negotiate the best rates; they don't depend on freelance professionals, they employ professionals in every one of their divisions. They pay high wages and they employ high quality people. They are mostly international so they have the advantage of being able to use the skills and knowledge of their colleagues overseas. They also have divisions which can offer advice on poster advertising, promotions and recruitment. How, then, is it possible to choose between these top agencies, each of whom offers everything an advertiser needs? Or perhaps, more importantly, why and when should we change our agencies?

"The answer is in advertising, as in most other businesses or sport, we have good runs and bad runs. In sport it is often said that someone has lost form. Why should they lose form? Why should an outstanding golfer suddenly lose touch? Why should a world beating tennis player begin losing matches regularly? Loss of form is so intangible, so difficult to pinpoint. The same happens to agencies, even the best of them, for no apparent reason. Suddenly they seem unable to come up with winning ideas. It isn't staleness. Lose one client and another steps in, eager to make use of the services of the outstanding agency. Why do they become stale with one client but not with another?

"It is simply that the think tanks concentrating on one particular product seem to dry up for a while, not for long, but for a while. It's loss of form. In time everything could change. An agency could be left in one year but rejoined two years later and give outstanding results.

"But nobody can wait those two years which is why we sometimes change agencies. Sometimes the creative genius, a very rare breed, leaves his company to start on his own. He could be worth following, as you said, Mike. During the last three or four years some of the largest accounts have been switched to agencies which were non-existent five or six years ago. Sometimes also, the giants get a little too fat, become a little too lax. They don't take criticism lightly. In fact, if they don't like taking criticism at all they are worth leaving.

"Then there are the giants who decide to revert to good marketing and, as they say in the USA, they come a-running, instead of demurring about taking on any new account. And if I continue in this vein," Drake went on, "I shall be stealing all your thunder, Mike."

"I don't think so," replied Harley. "And I shouldn't mind if you did." Then turning to Ashton he said, "You were highly critical of industrial advertising, but your company's campaigns have been successful so you told me. How do you account for that?"

Ashton said, "Last year we switched to an agency that specialised in industrial advertising. Firstly, the account executive handling our business knew very little about TV campaigns or poster advertising, but he was conversant with the needs of those who read the technical press and, of course, the trade press. He knew the media requirements, he knew our requirements, but he didn't begin to plan an advertising campaign until he had carefully studied our own marketing strategy and our sales literature. He insisted that the marketing strategy and the sales literature had to line up with the campaign; this, in spite of the fact that our allocation was quite small. He also arranged for a video to be made which we could show to consulting engineers and other specifying authorities. His objective, he insisted, was to increase the sales of our products. If, at the same time, he obtained extra goodwill, so much the better. That would be an extra benefit, but the objective was more and more orders.

"The campaign was very successful and in fact the advertising agency received an award for creative advertising.

"My advice to the industrial advertiser is to seek the help of specialist agencies. I don't think that requires any more elaboration."

Harley agreed and said, "It isn't easy for me to advise on the choice of an agency because I, perhaps, know too much of what goes on behind the scenes. But I'll try to be as factual as possible and provide a series of steps.

"Step one is to make a complete analysis of your own organisation so far as it applies to advertising. For example, who will be involved in giving advice, opinions, or decision making? The number should be kept to a minimum. Only one person should liaise between the company and the agency. Only one person should provide the basic information, possibly technical, to help the copywriters. Only one person should be the final decision maker. Decisions by committees should be avoided. No agency can operate effectively if it is continually faced with conflicting views. Agency personnel should not have to take sides.

"Step two is to define the advertising objective. Is it mainly to inform, to instruct, to create goodwill, to influence distributors, to influence retailers, to impress one section of a buying chain – which often applies when advertising industrial products – or to achieve more business, extra sales, higher turnover?

"Step three is to make a firm decision about the advertising budget. There can be no equivocation. Don't accept the agency's advice on expenditure; they must work within your budget and you must not increase expenditure to suit the plans of the agency. Once the budget is set you must adhere to it.

"Step four is to prepare a brief for selected agencies. The brief is based on the previous steps.

"Step five is to select several agencies for consideration; the number will depend on the budget. If there is a large budget, six leading agencies will be most willing to co-operate. If it is a small budget you may find that the larger agencies will not want to compete for your advertising campaign, but there are many small agencies that will go to endless trouble to get the business. However they usually use freelances and will not have complete control, for example, over time schedules. You have to be more careful in the selection of small agencies than with the larger ones. A good plan to discover the agency which would suit you best is to study press and magazine advertising and TV commercials. Some will be brilliant, some intriguing, some in the 'so what' category. Decide on which advertisements appeal to you most. There will then be no problem in finding out the agency used by the advertisers. A good idea is to contact the advertisers themselves; they are always helpful if you ask the right questions.

"There's the *Advertisers' Audit*, which lists agencies and their clients, but if you want to be certain that the agency is not working for a competitor or would-be competitor, the Institute of Practitioners and Advertisers should be contacted. They will send you a short list of agencies with no competitive clients.

"Step six is to approach an agency – by letter or telephone. My advice is to write a letter. Before attempting to judge the creativity of an agency you should find out whether or not you can work with them; whether they are efficient and enthusiastic. You can gain a first impression by the way they respond to your letter. If a reply is received by return, good! You can give eight marks out of ten for that. But deduct a point for each day's delay. If you don't receive a reply until five days later, five points are gone – it's not a very efficient agency. The content of the letter and its layout can also indicate the agency's attention to detail. Is the letter based on the you-we-I formula, or the I-we-you formula? The basic theme should be to satisfy client needs. Is the letter written in a friendly manner or is it cliché- and jargon-ridden? If the latter, it only deserves four out of ten marks.

"What then would merit ten out of ten? Why, an enthusiastic telephone call, of course, in response to your letter. The caller would obviously be keen to get your account. He or she should ask you when they can come to see you; not next week or the week after, but 'What time may I come today?'

"Never respond to that request. Don't allow them to come to you to ask you all the questions. You call on the agency, to discover how their receptionist greets you. Are you kept waiting too long before receiving attention or before an executive could see you? Is your subsequent discussion with that executive or account manager interrupted by telephone calls? That, again, shows lack of efficiency. Are you impressed by the standard of each of the offices you visited? They would be bound to show you one of their standard videos supporting their claims; did it impress you? Try to meet as many of their creative people as possible.

"Step seven is to draw up a shortlist of two or three agencies which you believe would best suit your requirements, having visited several. Invite them to make a presentation at fees to be agreed. Before they can do so they will want to carry out research and ask many questions. They will then be able to develop their ideas and present them to you. Your assessment of the presentation will be based on

(a) whether they interpreted your marketing plan correctly and produced creative ideas based on that plan
(b) their strategic approach to the objective
(c) careful evaluation of their media selections; sometimes the media suggested suits the agency better than the client
(d) ensuring that there are no hidden costs; this applies particularly to production costs which always escalate. You will be told that it is essential to do this, or that, at extra cost. If you stand firm you will be told: You have to pay a price for such a novel approach and every penny spent will be well worthwhile.

"Why take risks? My advice to advertisers when faced with the risk angle is: Resist it! Creative people, whether in films, TV or advertising, are rarely cost conscious. From the beginning insist that budgets must be adhered to. This cannot be emphasised too often.

"Step eight is the final selection. This is most difficult if all the agencies have made good presentations. Check with some of their clients and consider the following factors:

The agency response to your initial request for information.

Did they show continual enthusiasm throughout the negotiations?

Are you impressed by the account manager handling your advertising?

How do you rate the creative team?

Did the agency always keep to the time schedule?

Did they fully understand your marketing problems?

Did they study your competitors' advertising strategy to pinpoint weaknesses and strengths?

Were you impressed by their presentation?

Were you impressed by the video recording their past successes?

Are they cost conscious?

Are they logical thinkers?

Did they study your customer needs?

Did they show flair?

Did their message come out clearly in the advertisements or TV commercials?

Was there originality in the advertisements?

Did their copy avoid clichés?"

Harley paused to drink some water, then added, "Any advertiser who keeps to these suggestions based on experience, knowledge of advertising and my personal experience as an advertising agent stands a very good chance of succeeding with the agency of his choice."

14 More Problems

Pellew Grange management insisted on good time-keeping by their staff. If conference organisers had arranged definite times for tea, coffee or lunch, they would be strictly adhered to. Harley had relied on that when he had asked Susan Clifford to phone him at 4.05 exactly. He didn't want to phone Susan at the office and he asked her to ring him either from her home or from a callbox.

At 4.05 the call came through to Harley's bedroom. Picking up the receiver he said, "Hello, Susan."

"How did you know it was me?"

"I guessed. What news?"

"I saw Kenneth this morning as you suggested and told him that I was reconsidering the offer."

"You didn't, of course, tell him you had contacted me."

"Mike, you told me not to say anything. I don't break confidences."

"Sorry, Susan, I'm probably a bit on edge. At the moment, as I told you, if Jason thinks you are considering the matter he'll be much more open with you about the future and his intentions. What did he say this time?"

"He was happy that I was reconsidering the offer and he told me of the great future I'd have with Brooke & Dean. Apparently Corbett has decided that within a few years there will only be two or three big publishers; those companies that the Americans don't gobble up will be bought by British publishers. The small publisher has no chance whatever. Do you believe that, Mike?"

"No! He said the same to me, and it's generally accepted that the big publishers will get bigger and bigger through takeovers, but there will always be room for the small publisher provided he is highly efficient. Unfortunately the majority of small publishers are highly inefficient and they will disappear.

"If we get the right books – and we will, Susan – I promise you Harley's will succeed, because we'll be so efficient that booksellers will want to buy from us. They'll be asking other booksellers 'Why can't you be like Harley's? If they promise delivery, they deliver. If we order a special it's no problem to them, that special is delivered as well, right on time. And we meet with nothing but politeness when we telephone their offices. Yes, Susan, we shall succeed because we'll be so efficient in every direction. Even authors will get to know about us and will be prepared, perhaps, to forgo some special advantage offered by the larger publishers in order to be on our list, because we shall treat them as authors not just impersonal numbers ready to be praised when they do something good for us and condemned the minute something doesn't turn out quite right. You'll be glad you stayed with us, Susan."

There was no response.

"Susan, did you hear me?"

"Yes."

"Well, no comment?"

He could hear the audible sigh from the other end of the line, then Susan said, "Johnny Limmer telephoned me. He wants to talk to you urgently. I didn't tell him where you were but I said that if you telephoned the office I would ask you to contact him. He said he would be in his office until five o'clock and at home afterwards until seven o'clock. Here's his number . . ."

Mechanically, Harley wrote down the telephone number of Johnny Limmer, literary agent.

15 Promotions

There was no time then for a possibly lengthy discussion with John Limmer, agent for Harley's bestselling authors. Mike decided to telephone after seven o'clock.

He entered the conference room and said, "You won't be sorry for an early break tomorrow."

Ashton laughed. "We were just discussing how hard you've been working us and we had all thought it was going to be a nice semi-holiday."

Harley answered, "We are all dedicated marketeers discussing our favourite subject, so we have all enjoyed ourselves. Isn't that so?"

Everyone agreed that it was 'something they wouldn't have missed for the world', as Ashton put it.

Harley continued, "And here is your reward: I'm sure Ian's memo on pricing will be all-embracing. I suggest, therefore, that you read it early tomorrow morning. Ian is arranging for the night porter to deliver it to your bedrooms soon after 6 a.m. If you then annotate it with your comments I shall collect all the memos and make my own comments to you over breakfast."

"And that's good news?" said Drake.

"Wait for it, here it comes. I don't think pricing policy is open to discussion. There are set rules for pricing and it's only a matter of selecting the right rule for individual products or services. If, therefore, we all mostly accept the memo as read, we can cut out a session. And this means, now here's the good news, we can finish at lunchtime tomorrow if we complete direct marketing on time. And this, in turn, means there will be free time Thursday, from 1 p.m. onwards."

Like schoolchildren being given an unexpected holiday, the marketing directors clapped their hands joyfully.

Harley laughed. "That's agreed then. Now on to promotions, a definite growth area. It must be you, Colin, to start us off. You've been involved in so many promotions and sponsorships. Every packet of biscuits or box of chocolates seems to offer anything from a super holiday at a discount to a gardening tool for about 50p."

Drake said, "Promotion doesn't only mean giveaways. There are as many different forms of promotion as there are promotion agencies to advise on how to carry them out. Basically promotion puts pressure on retailers to increase their stocks heavily on the promoted products and it also changes loyalties. There are tens of thousands of people who buy products daily to take part in promotions and their actions can lead to a change of mind. A customer, for example, always buys brand *X* but, because of a promotion, switches to brand *Y*. That consumer may then remain with brand *Y*.

"And another aspect: big promotions with worthwhile prizes do impress and even enthuse retailers, leading to mass displays. Books are a typical example of this. Promote a book by an author signing and there will be many books on display, both before and after the signing. Isn't that right, Mike?"

Harley nodded his agreement.

"But you don't want me to go on listing promotions; I'm sure most marketing managers know them."

"There's no point in the book, Colin," Harley said, "unless we keep reminding marketing people of all options open to them."

"Very well," said Drake, "to begin with there are the usual free gifts. There are catalogues with a hundred or more products which can be engraved with a company's name; other catalogues list hundreds of inexpensive free gifts which can be redeemed by coupons or tokens.

"There are co-operative promotions. One example is Cunard's 'Fly Concorde to the USA and return via the QE2' at about the same rate as for a one-way journey. Another co-operative promotion was Lever's issue of 250 million tokens which could be exchanged for discounted rail travel.

"Taking dealers to conferences in ideal locations also comes under the heading of promotion.

"Summed up, advertising creates awareness, promotion creates demand. Is that the basic beginning you wanted, Mike?"

"Exactly!" replied Harley. "Now who wants to continue on the promotion theme?"

Cathy said, "I read somewhere that there is more money spent these days on promotions than on advertising, about £1,000 million or so. I wish they'd spend a little less on promotions and take more care of the way they are run."

"That," said Drake, "is a generalisation, Cathy, and one should never generalise."

"Maybe, but my view is that with all that money sloshing around some of the promotions could be better conducted. Although most of the large promotions are run for clients by promotion companies, if anything goes wrong and there is criticism, the blame falls on the client company.

"We so often read in the press stories of special offer products or free gifts against coupons collected being delivered months later because of shortages of stocks. The usual excuse is that 'demand was heavier than expected'. Management should not have to make such excuses. Rarely is an apology offered to a coupon collector who has sent off cash for a highly discounted product or a special gift which isn't delivered on time. In one case I read that the manufacturer of a tin opener which had been offered free to coupon collectors told a promotion agency after the initial supply had run out that they couldn't manufacture any more as they were now producing more profitable lines. That possibility should have been considered by the promotion agency or their clients before the promotion began.

"The promotion companies always claim that these are isolated cases. I can't prove them right or wrong, but even one mistake is one too many and it is up to the marketing directors to use a 'What if . . .' principle: 'What if this happens? What if that happens? What if supplies run out?' and to know how to placate customers who have not received their free gift.

"Don't you agree, Colin, that much more care should be taken to ensure that the demands can be met quickly?"

Colin Drake agreed, and went on "And one cause for consumer grievance is that the closing date for all such offers is not clearly printed on the labels or leaflets. The problem usually occurs when demand goes on and on. If there's a closing date no one can complain if gifts are not available beyond it.

"But I want to raise another factor which will, in some way, meet your criticism. You blame the client or the promotion consultants, but the latter are used to set up the campaign, suggest the gifts and lay down the rules. The redemptions are usually carried out by the handling houses. These fulfilment shops, as they are sometimes called, receive the tokens or coupons and distribute the free gifts, or check competition results. They also make payments to retailers who have collected tokens offering 10p off, or whatever. It's when the handling houses slip up that problems arise. If they fall behind with their work through wrong forecasting, for example, and they are overwhelmed by sudden demand, there's trouble all round. The consumers are upset, the main clients who receive the complaints are upset and the promotion consultants are upset.

"But even the handling houses have a lot to contend with. For example, in one case a handling house had to label individually, pack and despatch within a short period, 6,000 boxes of chocolates and there were five varieties on offer. Another handling house was asked to print 10 million letters and leaflets within a week. That's some going! It's really amazing that so few errors occur. There are over sixty handling houses, some of them owned by promotion consultants. The larger ones not only have the expertise and staff to redeem coupons properly, but also have the resources to pay out to retailers quickly, without submitting accounts to the promotion consultants and waiting for payment from them before reimbursing the retailers.

"They use computers to check the number of applicants per household. Some clients, when making special offers, lay down the rule that only one per household is allowed.

"So you see, Cathy, when Mrs Brown is annoyed because something has gone wrong with her application for a free gift, there is usually some excuse, if not a reason.

"Ideally, every campaign should be foolproof. That it is not is sometimes due to the client and the promotion consultants not bringing in a handling house early enough in the discussions."

"Fair enough, Colin," said Cathy, "but remember the letter to the publisher mentioned earlier. In that letter someone who complained about a gift was told that they shouldn't be upset because it was free. That reasoning clouds the mind of those offering such gifts. They tend to believe that the public is always wrong; that they have no right to complain if the free gift doesn't arrive on time, or doesn't arrive at all. The fact that they have collected a few coupons is neither here nor there. The object of promotions, surely, is not only to sell more goods, but also to retain customer goodwill and that means playing fair, even if it also means being over generous occasionally."

Drake said, "Yes Cathy, but sometimes problems arise which cannot be catered for. You may remember the many hundreds of people who queued for a prize in the *Daily Mail*'s Casino competition. Apparently, the competition had gone on longer than expected and there were so many prizewinners that instead of a fortune for the winner, each one of them received only a token amount. If the highly efficient *Daily Mail* and their promotional experts can slip up, so can others. But I agree, when things go wrong there must be apologies and everything should be done to put matters right."

Harley agreed, "I think that point has been made, so back to you, Colin."

Drake continued. "The point hasn't been made fully, Mike. The client is still held responsible for mistakes. It's the client's name that is at risk, not the agency's. Esso launched a scratch card game and had to withdraw it after a couple of weeks because the claims got out of hand. The *Yorkshire Post* ran into trouble when they offered a minimum prize of £250, not to be shared as is usual, due to a mistake in the bingo-type card. Claims ran into £1 million or more with no insurance cover. The *Yorkshire Post* had to rely on a rule allowing them to make changes in the payouts, which went against the grain for their fine management team. They had no alternative and the paper must have lost some goodwill. Cadbury apparently lost heavily when a syndicate cleverly broke their cash pot Typhoo game. The public have become highly sceptical of scratch cards and bingo-type games. That scepticism can only be overcome with much more careful vetting by client companies and games with odds of a million to one or so against winning should be scotched in favour of smaller, but more, prizes.

"Promotions usually offer only short-term benefits and do not replace advertising, which is often long term; but there can be a link between the two. For example, remember the delightful TV commercial picturing a puppy entangled in Andrex toilet tissue? Alongside that campaign there appeared on the Andrex packs an offer of donations to be sent to the Guide Dogs for the Blind Association on behalf of those collecting the tokens. That must have been worth a great deal in word-of-mouth advertising."

Drake paused. "Now let someone else take over."

Hayes began, "I'd like to touch on the need to insure against legal claims which might arise through a promotion going slightly adrift. My advice is always to seek the advice of a lawyer who understands all the legal implications and there are many in the promotional field, or perhaps minefield would be a better description. Mistakes can be very costly. There was once a John Player spot cash competition which the House of Lords decided was in breach of the Lottery Act. Imagine the cost of that exercise! Isn't that a point worth pursuing, Colin?"

Drake answered, "It certainly is! We do have such a legal adviser and here are some points which he has raised and which you may well think it worth including in the book, Mike:

"First of all, every word printed on the labels must be chosen with care. Even such a simple statement as '20 per cent off' might not be the correct wording to be used. Pint mugs were once on offer at a high discount, until someone discovered that they held slightly less than a pint. This resulted in a complaint to the trading standards officer which was upheld. The lesson is: Never give an exact measurement, always approximate.

"Here are some questions which should be asked before a promotion is launched:

Is the advertisement misleading in any way?
Are we making exaggerated statements?
Is the copy too emotive?
Would we win an argument with the trading standards officer? He knows all the constraints on promotions which apply to prize offers, draws, product descriptions even.

"Any medium-sized company entering the promotional field must be careful about the legal jungle, otherwise they could not only jeopardise the promotion but possibly the company itself.

"Now on to the next point. It may be asked, with the millions and millions of coupons issued, if they are all redeemed are such costly campaigns worthwhile?

"I was once told by the director of a correspondence course that they made their money on those, the majority, who started the course but never completed it, although they paid their fees in full. The same applies to most promotions. The coupons or tokens are collected, but the majority are not returned for redemption. I'm talking, of course, of consumer goods which account for about 55 per cent of all promotions."

Bruce Hayes said, "You can expect that percentage to lessen; there is an increasing number of banks, insurance companies and building societies getting into the promotion act."

After some discussion Harley said, "And sponsorship is also growing, not only in sport but also in books. There are cookery books sponsored by the Milk Marketing Board, and atlases sponsored by the AA or RAC. Books, unlike the usual promotional gifts of glassware, ashtrays and tablecloths, do have on them the imprint of the sponsors. And books on shelves are constant reminders of a company and its products. Of course I'm biased but I do suggest that many more marketing directors should consider sponsoring books; they're always winners.

"Cathy," Harley went on, turning to her, "tell us something about a promotion for a product launch. Before you moved into direct selling you sold through distributors and you once took about a hundred of them to Cannes. That was a big product promotion for a relatively small company, wasn't it?"

"Yes, but we were then, and still are, an organisation one step ahead of our competitors. We have succeeded partly because of our enthusiasm for testing out new ideas. The car people are the pioneers of the big launches with all the razzamatazz involved – showgirls, stunt men, you name it they've done it at some time or other. They want their dealers to be emotionally involved in an impressive experience. On returning home they will talk of the novel production, the fun and games, and also spread the news of the great new car.

"We employed a small agency made up of ex-TV and film people to organise our mini extravaganza as inexpensively as possible. We cut out the evening banquet, the type that is usually followed by champagne ad lib. Instead, we gave our guests a modest lunch and a buffet supper. We insisted that each section of the launch should be kept short and there would be no lengthy speeches, not even at the luncheon. The production was based on the Austin-Metro launch which, you may remember, was held aboard a cruise liner, the car emerging through a hole in the bulkhead.

"We did a skit on that. We had a ship replica with a hole in the middle and a handyman unsuccessfully attempting to push an air conditioning unit through the hole. That got the laughs and distributors must have wondered what was happening. Then, from the opposite side of the stage with a fanfare of trumpets, a cardboard airplane appeared and through an opening in its side our own unit came smoothly down the ramp.

"We announced that the one which had failed to leave the ship was a competitive unit – too big, too cumbersome, too heavy – while ours was sleek and could, if necessary, be moved easily from room to room. Our claim was: Twice the cooling at half the size.

"That met with tremendous enthusiasm! Our consultants had wanted us to employ a TV star as announcer, but we didn't agree. We did, however, have gorgeous girls handing out brochures and explanatory leaflets.

"We organised trips that were real fun. It was, on the whole, a great success and we learned a great deal from that promotion. We're going to do another for our sales force when we introduce a new range next year, although of course there are now tax problems with incentive conferences.

"This is what we learned from our first big promotion:

1. We should have taken more care with our initial briefing to our distributors. There were some slip-ups with timing and hotel accommodation; a misunderstanding regarding transport, and what could and could not, be charged to our account.
2. The lighting and filming went adrift on one or two occasions which was due to the fact that we had cut down on the number of experts needed to do the job properly. That proved to be false economy.
3. There were not enough lavatory and washing facilities adjacent to the conference rooms. We hadn't checked carefully enough.
4. The agency didn't give of their best, possibly because we kept cutting down on price. We should have vetted that agency much more carefully and also, perhaps, seen their point of view.
5. The press didn't turn up in force as we had expected,

possibly because there were two other product launches at the same time as ours. One was a fashion group whose boss was on an ego trip, the other, an Italian fridge company, whose bosses were throwing away lire like confetti. They got the coverage, we didn't. We should have had a full-time PRO."

Ashton interrupted, "But you still believe the promotion was a success?"

"Oh yes," enthused Cathy. "Most people hide their mistakes, I'm telling you about ours. Readers of the book will surely want to know what mistakes to avoid.

"It was a success, mainly due to our enthusiasm and hard work. Also we had a good product and won the dealers over by our almost loving care for each and every one of them. We sent each of them home with a present for his wife.

"In my opinion, although product launches overseas are expensive and mostly held by large organisations, smaller companies, determined to hit the market hard, will find that to win over distributors and salesmen a good promotion is better than lukewarm modest advertising campaigns.

"To sum up, all promotions should be under the control of the marketing director, but he must have a 'No-man' by his side – a pernickety accountant, or a crosser of t's and a dotter of i's assistant – someone who will check and keep on checking to ensure that everything will run smoothly. Nothing should be left to chance."

After some further questioning Harley said, "Thank you, Cathy. Now you might like to hear my experience of personality promotions. To use a personality, sportsman or film star, may or may not be a good advertising gimmick. It depends on the personality, but a link up with a star and a promotion does definitely achieve its objective.

"It's difficult in a book which will be published, possibly, eighteen months after completion, to name successful campaigns. I think it's safe to say that James Bond, the A Team, and anyone acting in 'Dynasty' or 'Dallas', associated with a product will definitely help to sell that product for a long time.

"Nervous inhibited men and women who really would like to be tough will buy almost any leather jacket or article of clothing promoted by the success of Dempsey and Makepeace. Children still follow the fortunes of Disney characters and will often insist on eating cornflakes only if the packet contains a Disney giveaway. Children are the greatest persuaders. If they follow Spiderman, anything Spiderman promotes is, so far as they are concerned, a buy. And are grown-ups any different? I've always been an avid follower of Henry Cooper, and willingly try any products he promotes."

Cathy interrupted, "I was in Harrods recently and bought a perfume called 'Forever Krystle'. Do you know I think I must have been influenced because Krystle Carrington is so lovely. I agree, none of us is immune from such promotions."

Harley said gallantly, "Krystle should be buying Cathy James skin preparations!"

"Thank you, kind sir!"

Harley grinned and continued, "From my experience, the advice I would give to manufacturers of toys, tee shirts etc., and biscuits, Colin – you have a biscuit promotion tie-up with Dainty Dolls – is either to get in quickly and take a gamble on some future success of a possible TV series, or not to go in at all. To come in too late is a sure loser. The gamble is whether a series or a star continues to be successful. Character merchandising is developing all the time and definitely creates a demand.

"Anyone want to comment on that?"

No one did, but Ashton added, "Are you going to cover exhibitions?"

Harley thought for a moment, then said, "No. To my mind exhibitions are sold, if that is the right word, on the idea that if you don't take a stand your competitors will and they will be the winners. Estate agents have nothing on exhibition operators when it comes to selling space. All the old selling tags are trotted out: 'There's not much space left'; 'It will be a problem getting a prime site later unless we can know quickly'; 'I've only got one corner site opposite the bar available. You'd better snap it up'.

"Some exhibitions are obviously essential, but many others are marginal. If you take a stand you will, of course, believe you have been successful. Everyone does. You'll kid yourself afterwards that you made some very successful contacts, which is exactly the same as a salesman making the excuse that he has met some good prospects that day instead of taking any orders. Incidentally, it's the salesmen who are the great persuaders when a marginal exhibition is up for consideration. Why? Because they like the change. They want to get off their territory for a while.

"The next point is that when you do take a stand at an exhibition, professional salesmanship is the essential ingredient for its success. It is selling that is usually so deplorable at exhibitions. Wonderful, enticing stands are useless if they are manned by exhibition layabouts. Poor management is to blame, rather than lackadaisical salesmen, who wouldn't be so non-caring if management had stricter controls."

When Harley paused Hayes said, "I'm sorry I can't be of much help in this session, but my knowledge of promotion is limited. In fact, I'm learning a great deal!"

"Your turn will come, Bruce," said Harley. "You and Cathy will, possibly, be the only contributors to our sales training session."

Harley turned to Drake. "It must be you, again, Colin."

Drake said, "I'd like to talk about a recent visit I made to the USA. In my opinion they are well ahead of us in promotional activities. I'm referring, again, mostly to promotions for the consumer outlets. Their promotion houses are into electronics in a big way. The 'in' thing, at the moment, however, is holography – three-dimensional photographs. At one time they were very expensive, but the costs have now been considerably reduced and I've seen some marvellous displays at Macey's, Gimbal's and several out-of-town hypermarkets.

"Holographs do, most definitely, promote products successfully. No one passes a three-dimensional picture without stopping and wondering. Another aspect is the linking of computers with moving messages. Instead of there being a series of messages repeated over and over, there can be a complete and instant change by using the computer link. There can be announcements of special offers or a last-minute free gift with a bottle of perfume, for example. Great stuff! Also they use video in stores much more than we do in the UK and these are most professionally produced; again, sure stoppers. In Britain, more often than not, someone in the office who knows something about cameras is given the job of putting together a video for a product message. For example, I've seen one showing a knife sharpener in operation, but it wasn't very effective. There's also a new on-shelf promotion. I saw a display of conserves; when a jar of jam was chosen, a recorded voice drew attention to other varieties further down the shelf."

Drake concluded, "A promotion consultant who wants to beat competition should employ an electronic wizard as a backroom boy who will produce electronic gadgetry which will attract attention by its originality. That production house would soon have a queue of marketing managers wanting to get in on the act.

"I really feel that's all I have to contribute on the subject. It's up to you now, Mike, to show us how to choose a promotion consultant."

Harley said, "I'll do that! And then we can call it a day."

He referred to some notes he had made, then began. "There isn't much difference between choosing an advertising agency or a promotion consultancy, except that no promotion groups could compare in size with the advertising giants. If you check at Companies House on the top dozen production houses, you'll discover that the average number of employees is probably about fifty and the profits are relatively small – well, they're high against turnover, but the turnover is relatively small. Anyone checking and believing that nothing succeeds like success would approach the most profitable of these consultancies. Alternatively, they could obtain a list of the twenty or more consultants – large, medium or small – from the Institute of Sales Promotion and an approach could then be made to a selected few. The same procedure would apply as for selecting an advertising agency. Write a letter to judge the speed of reply and the kind of response. Next visit the consultants and ask them to name some of their clients and ex-clients for you to contact. Ask clients and ex-clients to give you the pros and cons; the latter will, mostly, come from those who have changed to another promotion house.

"Here are some possible pros:

A dedicated group.
They never let us down.
They are innovative.
They use computers very effectively.
They have a research-based approach to all proposed ideas.
They offer a very comprehensive service.
They are good strategists.
They are professional.
They specialise in . . .
They continually come up with new ideas.
They don't suggest promotions which might annoy some consumers.

Only concerned with client benefits.
They are more expensive, but give a quality service.
They don't make excuses. If they make mistakes they put them right.
They can be relied upon.

"And now for the cons:

They became a little stale.
They talk of good promotions but don't carry through.
Too much like the Civil Service; not original enough.
They don't keep their promises.
They keep blaming the handling houses for errors.
They are too aggressive.
They are more thinking than doing.
They are a oneman band and when that one man's away, the band can't play.
They are very bad time keepers."

Harley paused, then continued, "There's little else that can be checked out. If the decision rests between two agencies, choose the one you can best work with."

Hayes asked, "Mike, how about telling us the best promotions with which you have been associated?"

Harley reflected. Then he said "Why? Promotion is all about innovation. Yesterday's ideas are not for the client who wants to get ahead of competitors. Imagine the response of a newspaper publisher told that bingo was a great success five years ago. But if you ask me how I would finally choose a promotion consultant I would answer, I'd look for someone high on creativity, who is also a great administrator. And on that high note we shall end what, I am sure we all agree, has been a very successful day."

16 First, the Bad News . . .

Mike had invited Cathy to join him and share a pre-dinner bottle of champagne in his room. Cathy, seeing the champagne nestling in the ice bucket, asked, "What are you celebrating, Mike?"

"Our being together again."

"But we're not."

"You're here, aren't you?"

"Yes."

"Then we're together again."

"We had lunch, remember, a month or more ago, when you told me about your new idea for a best-selling range of books."

"Right!"

"We were together then."

"But not in the bedroom!"

"Mike, you're impossible! Anyway, you should know from the past that champagne only makes me sleepy. And I'm not going to live with you again. Will you please get that into your head, Mike."

"Yes, Cathy. But remember, I never give up trying."

"Open the bottle and let's talk about something else. What's happening on the battlefront? Not that I'm really interested, because you won't tell me your plans."

"But you are interested, just the same."

"Of course!"

"I spoke to Susan during the tea break. Johnny Limmer contacted her. He wants to speak to me. I'm phoning him after seven."

"And who is Johnny Limmer?"

"A literary agent." Harley looked at his watch. "I'll ring him now and take a chance that he's home."

A few minutes later a breathless Limmer was saying, "I heard the bell ringing as I opened the front door. My den is on the first floor so I ran up the stairs. My doctor told me I shouldn't do that. I have a heart problem, you know. I told you about it."

There followed a description of Limmer's heart problem and his blood pressure problem, caused mostly by trying to placate difficult authors and publishers.

After listening to Limmer's problems for some minutes Harley said, "What did you want to speak to me about, Johnny?"

There was no reply.

"Johnny?"

"Sorry! I was taking my pill."

"Why?"

"Because I've had such a close relationship with the Harleys for years."

"Long may it continue!"

"I hope so. Unfortunately," a pause, and then he blurted out, "Lilian Greystone and Hugo Parkins are leaving you."

"Oh!"

" 'Fraid so," said Limmer, as if Harley had doubted the truth of the information.

"Why?" asked Harley. "They've both been with us for about twenty years."

"Because Brooke & Dean have made an offer for their next books. The manuscripts, as you know, are with me. I couldn't refuse on their behalf. You could never match the offer, Mike."

"How do you know?"

"Because I don't think any publisher would want to match it." He went on, "And neither author has had second book options in their agreements. You do know that, Mike."

"You didn't need to tell me that," said Harley. "I'll not fight for them."

"I'm sorry, but I promise you, if I get a winner I'll give you first option."

"I'm sure you won't Johnny, but don't worry. Take another pill. You may have more shocks coming your way before too long. Goodbye, Johnny."

Replacing the receiver Mike poured the wine and handed a glass to Cathy. "Let's drink to us," he said.

She didn't argue, but said quietly, "To us." After a few sips she said, "What was that call about?"

Mike told her.

"Corbett's pulling all the rugs from under your feet, Mike, you'll never survive the attack," she said. "Be sensible and sell out."

"Is that what you would do, Cathy?"

"No, I'm not as sensible as you, but what chance do you stand? His bookshops won't stock your books, not in any quantity anyway; he's taking your key staff away from you; and now your two best-selling authors, so you told me, whose books sell in millions I think you said, are leaving you. I think you've had it, Mike."

"Well, there's nothing more he can do."

"Except copy what you are doing now."

"Maybe, but it will take him time to catch up. I already have three management books under way."

"Please, Mike," she moved towards him and put her arms around him, "Please tell me what you will do. I do so want to help you."

"And so you shall! What are you doing Friday evening?"

"After we leave here you mean? Nothing!"

"Then have dinner with me and you'll hear all. There is one proviso: everything depends on a meeting I am having tomorrow afternoon. But I'm confident I shall win."

17 Memorandum on Pricing

On Thursday morning everything went to plan. Ashton's memo was received by each member of the team by 6 a.m. Discussions followed over breakfast and some changes were made.

Harley opened the first session. "I've made the alterations suggested and I'll hand out the copies of the revised memo." He did this, saying, "I'll check it with you and then we can move on to the only session of the day – direct marketing.

"After lunch I shall be returning to London and I'm not certain when I shall be back. I don't expect I'll be missed!" This was received by the usual music-hall routine: 'Oh yes you will', 'Oh no I won't'. After a few moments of this nonsense, Harley read out the memorandum.

MEMO from IAN ASHTON
on PRICING STRATEGY

Pricing is clear cut and needs little elaboration. It is for the marketing director in conjunction with other executives to decide on a pricing policy which must not be static. Pricing policies can be affected by changing conditions.

Before summarising the various pricing policies in general use, I shall list some of the objectives in pricing and some of the pitfalls which apply to most companies.

1. The objective is to make the highest profit in face of competition.
2. The profit must show an adequate return on capital employed.
3. It may be necessary on introducing a new range of products, when an immediate impact is required, to reduce profits temporarily before there is consumer acceptance.
4. A common error in the pricing of new equipment is to allow insufficient margin to cover after-sales service. Whatever assurances have been given by the product manager, they can be, and usually are, misguided. Even a quality fanatic cannot be sure of a product's operation under all conditions.
5. It is not good policy to increase profit margins by grinding down suppliers, insisting that they cut and cut again. If a supplier's price is unacceptable or obviously inflated other sources of supply should be sought. If, however, the price is competitive, then to demand further discounts can lead to the supplier cutting corners in his production. The buyer may then have to face loss of goodwill and additional service costs.
6. To kill off competition by price cutting a company has to be very rich. It can be done; it has been done; but it is not a good policy and rarely succeeds.
7. Sometimes a pricing policy depends almost solely on what the consumer expects to pay. A typical example is a Savile Row suit. One eminent tailor charges over £1,000 for a two-piece suit and his customers willingly pay that price.

   Farther down the road there is another eminent tailor who charges between £500 and £600 for a similar suit. His customers also willingly pay the price. The first tailor would not increase his trade if prices were cut by almost half and the second tailor would do no better by attempting to double the price.

Therefore, a pricing policy especially in luxury and semi-luxury goods need not be based on any fixed formula, but only on what the market will pay.

8. Some pricing policies allow for substantial discounts, the assumption being that their company's customers expect, and will fight for, such discounts. Although the costs of such discounts are always built into the price structure, the non-bargaining customers will fare worse than those who threaten to stop buying unless a large discount is allowed. Unfortunately the goodies are always beaten by the baddies, who get the better prices. If, however, the rule is that a discount is only given as a last resort and not as standard procedure, then that policy won't work at all. Salesmen will all too quickly offer the bigger discount to get the business. There is little company loyalty when discounts help to close an order. The solution is to offer incentives to salesmen for full price orders. This solution is abhorrent to those who believe that a salesman is paid to do a job and should carry out his company's policy regardless. They are right! But it still won't stop salesmen from giving discounts unnecessarily to get the business.
9. With a new product a decision has to be made whether or not to cream the market and make temporary excessive profits, or make a deep market penetration.
10. Prices of products can sometimes be kept down if there is a high subsequent demand for extras, spare parts etc. This applies to photocopiers, cameras, air filters and many other products.
11. There are two ways of initiating a price change. It can be swift, very much in the manner of the government introducing tax increases on tobacco and petrol, or it can be slow, to allow for rising sales before the increase takes place. The swift policy is standard practice in most direct selling companies, as it is for

cars. It does give the salesman a chance to obtain more sales, especially from dithering customers. There's nothing like a price increase to help a ditherer make up his mind.

12. Substantial price reductions to win a market or reduce stocks, as happened with computers, may sell more of those computers, but in the long term the gain is negligible. Usually it is a last resort. If there has already been product acceptance, nothing is to be gained by offering such large discounts to reduce stocks. Very few companies show a profit margin which can be slashed by 30 per cent and still leave something for the kitty. However this is a policy which sometimes has to be adopted if cash is urgently needed.
13. Unless in a specialised business, too high profit margins are an open invitation for others to enter that market and compete.
14. A pricing policy only works well if everyone, from the managing director downwards, keeps to budgeted expenditure. However, it sometimes happens that within three or four months of a budget being finalised there is a sudden influx of orders. The production manager then insists that he cannot cope without additional facilities that have not been budgeted for. Don't believe it. He'll cope. Sudden booms don't always last and can quickly be followed by a return to normality.

    Expensive journeys overseas or perhaps even more costly conferences might not be budgeted for. A marketing director should fight hard to restrain the over-enthusiasts whose solution to all problems is to spend more, budget or no budget. The rule should be: If it's in the budget, OK – that means it's covered by the pricing policy; not OK otherwise.
15. When dealing with rentals, take into account when

designing a profit strategy that cancellations will always be much higher than expected.

16. Don't buy business by offering exceptional prices for trade-ins. You cannot keep to a pricing policy if you keep changing the trade-in policy.
17. Very rarely do buyers purchase on the basis of price alone. This only applies if all similar products offer equal values. A pricing policy must take into account the benefits offered and if these are greater than those offered by a competitor, a higher price may be charged.
18. Pricing policy must allow for adequate discounts for distributors if the products are to be sold through distributors.
19. Without adequate profits there can be no positive cash flow, there can be no ploughing back, no development, no enthusiasm and no success.
20. Here are some problems to look for if profits are falling:

    production problems
    import problems
    cost problems
    shortage problems
    competitors' problems
    salesmen's problems
    supplier problems
    legislative problems.

    All of these problems can become serious if the pricing policy is not right.
21. Sometimes prices must be cut, but never make the decision because of salesmen's demands. First look at the quality of the salesmanship. That can be the problem, not prices.
22. One essential in pricing is to determine demand. The pricing policy will quickly go adrift if the demand is short of the forecast. Careful research before finalising a forecast is always essential.

23. When estimating costs before finalising a pricing policy, remember that they will always be higher than anticipated.
24. If a manufacturer does not invest in new machinery and uses antiquated systems, no pricing policy will work in the long run.
25. A certain way to failure of whatever pricing policy is decided upon is:

    to try to do everything at once
    to employ more salesmen than necessary to increase turnover
    to lower prices
    to increase advertising substantially
    to prepare expensive brochures
    to engage costly PR organisations, hoping they will be able to create new business quickly.
26. A higher price can always be demanded for quality products, but the proviso is that they must always be high-quality products, not figments of the production director or the advertising manager's imagination. If a product undoubtedly does last longer, has less breakdowns, is more competitive than other brands, when an honest twenty-four hour a day service is offered and the product meets all the demands of a buyer, prices can be upgraded.

The price of a product or service will depend on marketing objectives. These could be:

to maximise volume
to maximise turnover
to maximise market share
to maximise profits
to develop a particular market image
to cream off the most profitable parts of the market
to flood the market
to hit the competition
to get established in the market.

There are broadly three different approaches to setting prices: the economist's, the accountant's and the marketing man's.

THE ECONOMIST'S APPROACH

Economics is based on the theory of supply and demand. In the long run the market price of any product, commodity or service must be acceptable to the seller and the buyer.

Equilibrium pricing means equating supply and demand. If demand exceeds supply the price is increased, while if supply exceeds demand prices are decreased. A good example is the bookmaker whose objective is to have a balanced book at every race. If horse *X* is a favourite at three to one and there is a rush of bets, the odds are decreased to two to one, while the odds on other horses will be increased and continue to increase, to attract the punters, or be decreased if the demand becomes too great. This pricing policy will result in a balanced book. The bookmaker cannot lose and must make a profit if the favourite loses. That is equilibrium pricing.

THE ACCOUNTANT'S APPROACH

Cost-plus pricing obviously means taking the cost of production plus an extra for profit. The most common variations are:

Variable Cost-Plus Pricing This consists of totalling only the *variable* costs of providing the product and using this total as the cost base, adding a certain percentage to cover *fixed* costs and provide for profit.

Production Cost-Plus Pricing The actual *production* cost total is used as the base, after apportioning all production overhead expenses to the various units of output. A certain percentage is then added to cover selling and administrative expenses and to provide for profit.

Total Cost-Plus Pricing *All* the organisation's costs are allocated to units of output, using absorption costing techniques where appropriate. The percentage to be added then only has to provide for profit.

Although cost-plus pricing is the most commonly used pricing system, it does suffer from the defect that it takes no account of the market.

Contribution pricing relates the total contribution, i.e. sales less *variable* costs, earned at different prices/sales volumes to the fixed costs of running the business; this way the profits which will be earned at different prices can be estimated. A pricing decision can then be made based on the company's profit objectives and relative risks and rewards of selling at different prices.

Opportunity cost pricing is used where there are, at least potentially, different mutually exclusive opportunities to sell the same product or service. The price quoted is based on the cost to the supplier of *not* being able to sell or utilise the product or service elsewhere.

The Marketing Man's Approach

For every product there is a price which the market will bear. The different pricing systems used are:

Comparative pricing or *Competitive pricing*, where prices are set according to what competitors are charging. It may be policy to charge either the same, less or more. Whatever the policy, it must be linked to the company's marketing strategy.

Customary pricing, where the market has established a set of prices or range of prices for a product.

This pricing policy depends on cost-cutting awareness for its success.

Differential pricing is based on the technique of market segmentation. Different types of customer or prospect can be sold in different ways and at different prices. Price is only one part of the total offer and differential prices must be justified by an effective marketing plan.

Value-in-use pricing is where prices are set by estimating how much the product is actually worth to the customer in terms of gain or saving of money. This may bear no relation at all to the cost of the product.

Psychological pricing is designed to have a particular psychological impact on customers. For example, to make the price appear lower than it really is, to make the quality seem higher than it really is, or to imply exclusivity.

Conclusion

I have tried to give a précis of pricing strategies. There are, of course, many intricate formulae based on mathematical calculations and computerised programmes. Basically, however, they cannot vary a great deal from the main pricing policies and the attendant problems which have been shown.

IAN ASHTON

18 Direct Marketing

At 9.45 a.m. discussions on the pricing policy outlined by Ian Ashton ended. Harley looked at his watch. "We have three hours to debate direct marketing. We'll cut out the coffee break. Everyone agree?"

All agreed, so Harley rang reception and cancelled the coffee. Then he said, "We have all had some experience of direct marketing, sometimes possibly without realising it. I shall try to define the activity and then the sections we'll cover. Direct marketing, in my opinion, is when sales opportunities are created by the direct contact between seller and buyer. Here are some examples:

"An advertisement inviting readers to take piano lessons, or become successful writers; to complete and return a coupon; to order a product; to send for details of holiday apartments; to save with a building society . . .

"A telephone call intended to close a sale with the person accepting the call or to set up an opportunity with the same objective.

"A leaflet delivered through the door, inviting subscriptions to a local newspaper or the hiring of a minicab, the engaging of a builder, plumber, double-glazer . . .

"A letter or brochure inviting orders for a magazine, coverings for chairs, materials for curtains . . .

"Selling from catalogues, possibly the most popular of all direct marketing activities, and all forms of direct mailings.

"As we have chapters covering advertising and telephone usage I think we should now concentrate on selling by direct mail."

Harley continued, "Direct mailing is the provision of information on goods or services to enable potential buyers to order through the post, or to pave the way for a salesman to call and it can be used most effectively by those in specialised fields. Products with more general appeal such as tobacco, foodstuffs and drinks are more suited to press and TV advertising. The six factors which, in the main, determine the success of a direct mail campaign are as follows:

1. Testing before a full campaign is unleashed. There may have to be a series of tests to determine which type of mailing will bring in the best response.
2. The quality of the mailing list.
3. The effectiveness of the sales literature or letter.
4. The accuracy in measuring returns to establish whether or not the campaign is effective.
5. A computerised filing system to enable a strong list to be built which can be targeted again and again. Those who buy by direct mail will nearly always continue to do so.
6. The continuation of the campaign. One-off shots are rarely as effective as a series of mailings to the same target audience.

"That's enough of basics. Now for a salutary thought: possibly 90 per cent or more of all general mailings, as against specific mailings, go straight into the waste paper basket. The aim for the direct marketing manager is to cut that percentage so that only 70 per cent of the mailing goes into the basket. The balance is glanced at, and following the glance, possibly a 5 per cent request is made for more information or maybe even an order is sent.

"In my opinion, most of the 90 per cent that end up in

the waste paper basket deserve their fate. The aim of the direct marketing manager is to hold the interest of the overworked recipient, who does not take kindly to a post consisting mainly of mailing shots. It is these people who have to be persuaded to read and take action. So much depends on the presentation of the mailing pack, its specific appeal and its persuasiveness.

"Now," said Harley, "let's settle a controversial point by asking Colin a series of questions:

"Colin, when you receive letters at your home address do you open the envelope and at least glance at the contents, regardless of whether the envelope is franked or not, regardless of whether the stick-on label gives the game away and indicates a computer list?"

Drake thought for a moment then said, "My wife opens most of our mail and she definitely slits all the envelopes and reads the contents. If I get the letter first I glance at the envelopes and know instinctively which contain personal letters and which are mailing shots – and yes, despite this, I open them all and scan the contents.

"Good!" said Harley. "I believe most of us act this way. Therefore when mailing to homes it doesn't much matter how the envelope is addressed, how it is typed, what class postage is used, or whether or not the senders' names are printed on the envelopes. Now Colin, here's another question: At the office does your secretary open and sort your mail for you?"

"No, not always. She may be out of the office when the mail arrives. Often I'm at the office before her and I always give priority to seeing what's in the mail."

"Right! When your secretary sorts through the letters does she separate the direct mail shots from the personal mail?"

"Yes."

"And do you look at all the mailing shots?"

"No. But she does and she would draw my attention to any which she felt would interest me."

"Is that all, Colin? Please think carefully."

"Well, I suppose if a particular mailing intrigued her, interested her, she would show it to me anyway and say, 'That's good, isn't it?' or something like that."

"That's fine," said Harley. "So, as far as your secretary is concerned, it doesn't really matter how the name and address on the envelope is typed."

"Hold it! You're wrong there. If a mistake has been made, for example if my name is spelt incorrectly or my title isn't right or the company's name is misprinted she, being marketing-minded, will be highly critical and the envelope with its contents will go into the waste paper basket pretty quickly."

Harley said, "But if the name and address etc. are correct, she will still open the envelope regardless of whether these details are hand-written, typed, or have been spilled out of a computer. Is that correct?"

"Yes."

"Good! Now for the next point: When you open the mail yourself are you influenced by the computerised name and address, the flimsy envelope, or the senders' name printed on the outside?"

Pausing for a moment, Drake answered, "Yes, if I can see through the envelope and recognise that the appeal is from yet another office supplies company or photocopy group or advertising agency, I drop it pretty quickly into the waste paper basket without bothering to slit the envelope. And if the sender's name is on it, that can go into the basket even quicker."

Harley said, "Then you never give the sender a chance to persuade you to consider changing an office supplier, using a different employment agency, or whatever?"

"Right!"

"Now we all know why such a large percentage of envelopes containing the creative thoughts of direct mail specialists go unread. Does anyone disagree with Colin's comments?"

They all agreed that they took similar action.

"Why, then," asked Ashton, "do so many companies print their names on the envelopes?"

Harley replied, "So that non-deliveries can be returned, I suppose, or they may consider it good advertising. By the way, I'm not going into the realms of slogans on envelopes, I'm only covering direct mailing.

"A prime lesson, therefore, is that envelope addressing etc. doesn't much matter for mailings to the home, but for business mailings a good quality envelope should be used. Names and addresses should be carefully checked and the company's name, i.e. the senders' name, omitted from the envelopes.

"The next question is: What should be the contents of the mailing shot? I'm going to leave out the gimmicks. The backbone of the majority of mailing shots is the letter and brochure, catalogue, programme or photograph.

"Firstly, it must be decided whether or not a brochure is necessary. Will the letter alone achieve the objective?

"The answer is, most definitely yes, if the letter not only keeps to the rules but is creative and appealing.

"The next question is: Should the letter be long or short? If a brochure is enclosed in the envelope, then the shorter the better.

"In the USA I have seen excellent letters used by direct selling organisations of three pages or more. These long letters achieve their objectives because they maintain interest throughout. In the main, however, direct mail letters should be kept as short as possible. The aim is, in as few words as possible, to grip the interest of the recipient and persuade him or her to take action.

"To write a compelling sales letter the first action is to review the important selling points of the product or service, then extract the features which will be of interest to most recipients of the letter. Give sound reasons why actions should be taken by the recipients; never try to be too clever; avoid humour entirely. Avoid all clichés and out-of-date phrases; stress only one or two greater benefits and one or two subordinate benefits at the most. Once again, the total concept of the letter must be based on the *you-we-I* formula. *You* will benefit because . . . *We* will, because of our expertise, ensure that more benefits accrue to you . . . *I'll* telephone you tomorrow.

"Although the telephone close can only be used for small mailings, closes used for bulk mailings can in most cases be improved. So often the conclusion of letters reads: 'Please write for further information', when a better action ending would be: 'A call from you will enable us to prove very quickly how *X* can improve your . . .'

"Direct mail letter-writing technique is an art well worth studying, especially by marketing directors. Even copywriters of direct mail houses may not be all that good, therefore when examples of letters are submitted to the marketing director he should analyse them carefully and improve them wherever possible."

Harley continued, "There are some people who believe they can write a good direct mail letter in a matter of an hour or so. The experienced creative writer will only provide a first draft in that time and for the rest of the day there will be more drafts to follow. It may take days before he is satisfied with the final results. Every sentence will be reviewed and revised, if necessary, to strengthen it. Every word must be considered. Is that word necessary? Could a shorter word be used? Could a better word be used? Finally he should seek the advice of others. Criticism should be invited because even the expert cannot always see his own faults. You will find, if you make this study, that 50 per cent or more of direct mail letters are ill-conceived and badly written."

Ashton interrupted. "The predominant interest our readers are going to show is the profitability of direct mail. Don't you think that is a priority?"

Harley agreed. "You're right, Ian. Direct mail can be a highly profitable form of marketing because:

it is selective
it can be produced quickly
it can be used by the smaller companies unable to finance newspaper or TV advertising
it can be tested economically, often not possible with other forms of advertising or direct selling
it only competes with other letters on a desk or table requiring to be read, not with other forms of advertising or direct selling
it can have a personal appeal
it can be judged by immediate results.

"There are also clear indications as to whether a campaign is successful or not. A blind shot, the indiscriminate posting of a large number of letters or leaflets to every possible buyer in an area, is considered successful if a 1 to 2 per cent response is received. Most blind shot mailings will be discarded, although glanced at, because at that particular time the recipient is not interested in the product or service offered. He may well have been interested a month earlier and could be again three months later, but not on the day the mailing is received. Specific mailings, however, can bring in much higher returns.

"If a mailing is badly planned and has little appeal – is too gimmicky or crude, the copy ambiguous or the brochure lacking in dynamism – a blind shot or a specific campaign will bring only a negligible response."

Harley invited comments, but there were none, so he continued. "The objective of a mailing is always to influence minds. A campaign for mailing the medical profession can never result in even one direct sale, but it can persuade a doctor to prescribe a drug and that is an indirect sale. Whether the aim is direct or indirect sales or a subscription to a charitable fund, a mind has to be influenced to take action. That is selling.

"Specific objectives could be:

to pave the way for sales calls
to make a direct sale
to create a need
to secure information from dealer or retailer
to give information to distributor or retailer
to tie in with an exhibition, special promotion or advertising campaign
to obtain service contracts
to educate equipment users
to sell extras
to increase distribution
to market research
to obtain book subscriptions
to create demand for new products
to get products specified by architects, consultants . . .
to maintain contact with customers between calls.

"There are many other objectives for a direct mail advertising campaign and its basis will always depend on its objective. Is it to be a selling campaign, an informative campaign, a promotional campaign?

"Having made the decision, the planning can start. There are four main factors to be considered:

(a) the mailing list
(b) the presentation
(c) the completion
(d) the testing.

"The best sources for mailing lists are customers and prospective customers. The old adage, 'use your users', applies as much to direct mail as to person to person selling. Regular mailing of customers will bring better results than can be obtained from a blind shot campaign. Prospective customers, i.e. buyers who have shown interest but have not placed orders, are also potential buyers from mailings. A customer and prospect list should always be kept as up-to-date as possible. Movement of personnel, closing down of businesses, changes of address mean that it will never be accurate on a day-to-day basis however well updated it may be, although it will still be the best possible list.

"For blind shots, lists of possible buyers can be compiled from telephone directories, trade directories, credit rating directories, business registers, trade association lists and advertising. Because much of the information in directories is published some twelve months after it has been compiled it goes out of date quickly. As there is always approximately 20 per cent wastage, they are only likely to be 80 per cent correct.

"Now on to list brokers. Brokers sell lists covering practically every trade or profession. A list broker will often save the time of analysing directories and can usually provide a list to suit exact requirements. The credentials of the list broker should, however, be examined carefully. If lists are not kept up-to-date, there could be as much as a 25 to 30 per cent margin of error.

"Finally there are the direct mail agencies, which should provide these services:

- the list
- designs and copywriting for letters or leaflets
- preparation of long-term campaigns
- facilities for electronic typing, facsimile printing, word processing or litho printing and matching in of names and addresses
- computerised mailings
- modern inserting and labelling facilities
- up-to-date folding equipment

modern techniques for flat wrapping
a printing service
a design promotion service

"When selecting an agency you will want to know:

(a) what services they offer
(b) which services they carry out themselves and which are subcontracted by them
(c) whether they employ skilled copywriters – suggest meeting one of their copywriters to check his ideas
(d) if they employ staff with creative skills; examine some of their work for originality
(e) whether they pass credit for undelivered letters if returns are due to errors in their mailing lists.

"Next, consider the presentation of your mailing package. What will influence buyers, or prospective buyers, to ensure that they respond to your shot while, perhaps, ignoring others? That is the crux of a campaign. Even a near perfect list will bring little response if a presentation is colourless, unimaginative, lacking in appeal and does not arouse immediate interest. The presentation can be based on:

the stunt or gimmick
the booklet or leaflet
the letter.

"A gimmick may succeed once in a hundred times when mailing to industry, although it has a much higher rate of success when mailing to householders. The gimmick secures attention, but can detract from the message. The keen buyer may be amused, but he can also feel that his ability as a buyer is being denigrated. These are some of the gimmicks used in the past:

a length of string to suggest that there are no strings attached to the offer

a length of string already knotted as a reminder to place an order
a pin for pinning a cheque to the order
a bill from a nursing home to alarm a prospect into appreciating the need for extra insurance to cover such bills
a wedding ring – let's tie things up!
an aspirin – 'We save you headaches'
a tape to relay a message
a magnifying glass to suggest the improved results that will follow taking action
a piece of chalk for chalking up greater success.

"Other gimmicks include unusual paper sizes, trick folds to enable a prospect to build a cardboard model of the product, quizzes, lucky numbers, special offers, pictorial appeals, strip cartoons, photographs and humorous drawings.

"Sending out gimmicks can be costly. Even one extra fold in a letter increases the cost, as does any enclosure. Gimmicks, therefore, should be used sparingly and very rarely apply when selling to industry.

"Basically all booklets or leaflets are designed to tell a story with a beginning, a middle and an end. The modern trend is to print a teaser on the cover of the leaflet to intrigue, without giving precise information; the aim being for the recipient to want to read the full story on the inside pages.

"Brochures or booklets are rarely used except by large companies who can afford goodwill mailings. The cost is too high for a standard mailing. If it is decided that a brochure or booklet should be used, this should be planned by a professional designer and the copy written by an advertising copywriter. But most important of all is the letter.

"The letter is an integral part of the presentation. A well-written letter is more effective than any brochure, leaflet or gimmick. The majority of recipients will read a letter because it is more personal than any other form of sales literature.

"A leaflet, however, can be colourful, descriptive and diagrammatic and can visually pinpoint a problem and its solution. Therefore it may be thought that a combination of letter and leaflet is preferable to either of them alone. Unfortunately a leaflet can detract from the appeal of a letter and the personal impact can be lost. Also, if a powerful leaflet tells the whole story, there is little need for a letter. The letter can only draw attention to the leaflet and a lengthy, descriptive letter implies that the recipient is so moronic that he can't see for himself that a leaflet is enclosed.

"It is time wasting to expect the recipient to read a long letter telling the full story and then urge him to read the full story again printed in the leaflet. If a letter is used, it should be short, create confidence and highlight one important benefit to be found amongst others in the leaflet.

"Usually it is preferable to use a well printed leaflet alone, or a letter alone, always remembering that the leaflet can sell while the letter can usually only generate an inquiry. A well thought out letter has a greater impact, so I'd better give you a letter checklist.

1. Is the objective clear?
2. Has readership been clarified?
3. Is the letter directed towards that readership?
4. Is the opening merely a preamble, or does it arouse interest?
5. Have the facts been verified?
6. Does it deal, in the main, with one project/product/service only?
7. Has it been edited for qualifying sentences, over long sentences, complex sentences?
8. Is it grammatically correct?
9. Does it punch home vital words?

10. Has it 'you' appeal?
11. Does it stress benefits?
12. Have as many 'I's' as possible been cut out?
13. Is it free of hackneyed phrases?
14. Does it create confidence?
15. Does it create desire?
16. Does it show understanding of the reader's problems?
17. Is there an overuse of superlatives?
18. Is it the kind of letter you would like to receive?
19. Have such words as 'hope', 'trust', 'feel' been deleted?
20. Does it tell the reader exactly what you want him to do and does it make it easy for him to do it?"

Harley paused a moment, then added, "A second colour should not be introduced in the body of the letter; it rarely adds to the appeal. Second colours may be used when letters are printed in leaflet form. This type of mailing is a favourite for promotions for magazine subscriptions.

"Advice should be sought on the use of colourful envelopes, picture envelopes or envelopes on which messages may be printed. For the majority of campaigns it is advisable to enclose a reply-paid card. Consideration must be given to its design so that it can be co-ordinated with other sales material. Reply-paid cards may be colourful and attractively designed, as may order forms and gift forms. The recipient may even be invited to initial a letter and return it in a pre-paid envelope to obtain further information.

"There is one point which is often overlooked: no mailing is complete until action has been taken by the recipient – an order signed, a request for further information to be sent, or an enquiry card completed. The success of a campaign, however, can be marred by the inefficient handling of inquiries received.

"The following rules may be applied:

1. An enquiry register should be designed to include all information: date of arrival of enquiry, date of despatch of letter to client acknowledging its receipt, date information passed to salesman, salesman's report on enquiry. Additional information required might be credit rating, previous purchases made and the possibilities of other outlets.
2. This register must be referred to regularly, to check on the need for further action: letter, telephone call, personal call. The results of such actions must be noted in the register.
3. Every enquiry must be answered, if possible, the same day it is received, but certainly no longer than twenty-four hours later.
4. If the enquiry is passed to a salesman he must give it immediate attention. If he is unable to contact the enquirer within forty-eight hours he must advise head office, so that other arrangements can be made for contacting the prospect.
5. A stereotyped duplicated letter should never be sent, however large the response. If necessary, a well printed form card may be used, giving the date by which full information will be posted.
6. If a follow-up is to be handled by mail or telephone, a planned sequence must be adhered to: dates when follow-up letters are to be posted and a person nominated for follow-up telephone calls.

"The next requirement is testing. One advantage of direct mail is the simplicity and inexpensiveness of testing each shot. There should be no important mailings without testing. The only returns that are of value in testing are direct orders, direct enquiries, requests for samples, demonstrations etc. Letters acknowledging receipt or letters advising of no interest at the moment should be ignored. The following can be tested:

first class mail or second class mail results
whether to personalise letters by matching in the list
the copy for the letter
reply devices
whether samples should be included
the number of enclosures
whether a sample be sent or whether it is better to urge the recipient to take action and write for a sample.

"Tests have shown that in some cases it is better to get a request from the recipient for further information so that a salesman can call, rather than enclose a sample in the first instance.

"If a brochure is to be produced for mailing or a do-it-yourself kit designed, the fixed cost of production is so high that it rarely pays to print in limited numbers. Therefore it is not always possible to test the copy or design of brochures. The exception is when the ultimate mailing is in the hundreds of thousands.

"A test campaign should be approximately 10 per cent of the mailing, with a minimum of 1,000. If the shot is to be over 100,000, a 5 per cent test will be adequate.

"These are the rules for testing:

1. All tests must be carried out at the same time and under the same conditions.
2. The test list must be representative of the whole list.
3. Don't under- or over-test. It's useless to mail 300 or 400 letters to test a mailing of 100,000, but 100 letters might be sufficient to prove whether a specific personal letter can pull in results.
4. Follow the test quickly. When the results have been evaluated there must be no delay before the campaign

is mounted, otherwise unknown factors may creep in: weather, holidays, strikes . . .

5. However certain you may be of the brilliance of a campaign, however adamant the direct mail house is that you have a winner, always insist on a test.

"Direct mail can be launched quickly and the whole of the country can be covered within twenty-four hours if necessary.

"It can be timed to suit the requirements of the potential buyers. For example, summer wear during summer months, heating during winter months, sportswear to tie in with sporting events – Wimbledon, open golf championship, Henley etc.

"A blanket cover can bring the message to every likely prospect. It can boost the morale of a sales force and keep alive those small accounts which are too costly to contact by a personal call. It gives relatively inexpensive continuity of approach. Few companies are too large or too small to benefit from a direct mail campaign. Direct mail is that extra salesman, to bring in that extra profit."

Harley stopped to sip some water and said, "Now who would like to take over?"

"None of us," answered Drake. "You haven't completed your task yet. You haven't given us your views on enclosures."

Harley grinned. "I believe you want me to do all the work while you're taking it easy. I promise I'll make time for your contributions. OK then, my next contribution will be on enclosures.

"Priority is, of course, quality. Very few marketing directors are designers. If a brochure or leaflet is to be included with the mailing, the marketing director may supply the copy but he should employ a designer to lay out the leaflet effectively. There's little more I can add on the policy of enclosures, but there is one concern that every marketing executive has to consider: too many of them believe they are saving money if they enclose everything in the mailing shot, including the proverbial kitchen sink. If there are ten different units, there must be ten different leaflets. That is an incorrect concept.

"When we receive a mailing shot which interests us sufficiently to make us want to know more, we are put off if we are faced with a dozen or more leaflets offering us alternatives."

Ashton said, "I can give you an example of that mistake. Only last week I received a mailing from a very well-known hotel. It included several separate leaflets covering their restaurant *A*, their restaurant *B*, their coffee shop *C*. There were also two more leaflets detailing their banqueting facilities, both large and small; there was another leaflet on accommodation and yet another on the garage facilities. I only looked at them because the hotel manager is a friend of mine.

"One leaflet would have been sufficient to describe their magnificent restaurants and my delight on savouring the superb food provided by their master chef . . ."

Harley nodded. "Thanks, Ian, and to show my gratitude to you, you may now take over. What I want each of you to do is to consider other concepts of direct marketing and, of course, add to the basic principles I have already outlined."

Ashton said, "One question I want to ask you, Mike, is what is the best day for mailings to be despatched and received?"

Harley answered, "There used to be good postal deliveries, but today we can't rely on them. It's no use posting second-class on Friday and assuming that delivery will be on the following Monday. But if posts are more or less guaranteed, it's usually considered best for home mailings to arrive on a Saturday. This gives the family the weekend to read them and if it happens to be a wet weekend, they could be read avidly. To business houses, however, factories, offices etc., the best day to receive mailings is either Tuesday, Wednesday or Thursday. Also there should never be office mailings during bank holidays and, possibly, August as well.

"Sorry I can't be more specific, Ian, but these days not so much thought is given to the timing of mailings."

Ashton replied, "Thanks! Now for my last point. When we mail regularly we change our notepaper headings and even the type of paper we use. We have found that prospects and customers are apt to glance at the company's heading, believe they know what the letter is about and the mailing shot goes into the waste paper basket. That's all from me at the moment."

Harley looked inquiringly at Drake, who accepted the non-verbal invitation and said, "The point I want to make is, if possible, always make a free offer. Free offers are rarely thrown into the waste paper basket. It's surprising how even top executives like a free fountain pen or diary or the opportunity to win a big prize. But I agree with you, Mike, avoid gimmicks and stunts.

"I had a mailing the other day where the envelope measured 24 inches square. It annoyed me and it cluttered the desk. I didn't read it.

"My next point is that a mailing followed by a salesman's call has a greater effect than relying on direct response by post alone. It's a good opening for a salesman to say, 'You have, no doubt, read our letter' . . . The reply will probably be, 'What letter?' – which immediately gives the salesman the opportunity to create interest and confidence.

"That's all. I think it's your turn, Cathy."

Cathy James began, "We do use direct mailing extensively. We have massive mailings about once a year and regular specific shots when we are most careful to match up names and addresses with the type face. Also we give a lot of thought to our leaflets. They must stress benefit after benefit.

"Experience has taught us that certain territories are not worth covering so far as our salesmen are concerned. The cost of a sales force today is so high, with expenses, cars, insurances and so on, that if they can only make one or two calls a day on a sparse territory, the effort is too costly. But we have customers on those territories and we mail them regularly – and those mailings are always followed up by telephone calls. There must be co-ordination between those responsible for mailings and the sales office. Writing and telephoning make an ideal direct marketing policy."

Harley said, "We're doing fine! It must be your turn, Bruce!"

Hayes answered, "I haven't very much to contribute, but we have found that when mailing managers and top executives a good way to get a response is to enclose a questionnaire, the basis of which is to help us establish client needs.

"We usually offer a free gift for its return, something simple like a diary or a map. It's surprising the response we get and from that response we are definitely able to define client needs. Of course, we can add more names to our mailing lists and, as we keep stressing, mailing lists are all-important. Not much of a contribution, Mike, but it does work."

"A good approach," said Harley; then turning to Drake added, "It must be your turn again, Colin. You probably use direct mail most of the time."

"Yes we do and as mentioned during our research session we mail samples and free offers and we find that the direct response is far better than from advertising. Perhaps it would be more correct to say that we are able to check the response from mailings more accurately. We also mail our wholesalers and distributors regularly, but after listening to your advice, Mike, it's probable that we have never given enough thought to that project. Our mailings have been much too general, too ordinary. You know the sort of thing: price lists, brief details of advertising campaigns etc. No, not ordinary – bloody awful! But from now on I shall give instructions that all mailings must have 'you' appeal, contain heaps of benefits, arouse interest and, of course, have good closes. I'm afraid we've taken our customers too much for granted in the past and believed that sending out these lists was enough. We must take much more interest in our users and from now on, we shall.

"To make a switch, I'd like to talk about guarantees. While consumer legislation covers all products and services and is really all that is needed, our customers still prefer to have our guarantees as well, and they like to see them printed on every packet, in every leaflet and in every direct mail shot. Products guaranteed to give satisfaction or money refunded or goods exchanged are still a good confidence builder."

"May I interrupt there?" said Cathy.

"We also believe in giving guarantees, but our customers have to return a card to have these guarantees confirmed. Obviously this doesn't affect their statutory rights, as you mentioned earlier, Colin, but the return of the card does enable us to add to our mailing lists and that, as we've all said, is so important. That's all, so back to you, Colin."

Drake said, "We, in the consumer field, all use direct mailing to offset the demands of the multiples, superstores and big buyers. Sometimes they almost threaten our salesmen that products will be removed from the shelves unless we give this or that concession. The antidote is direct mailing. We mail householders with our special offers, price discounts and gifts for those products that the retailers threaten us they will no longer stock. This mailing invariably brings results, because consumers put pressure on the multiples and they then have to stock the product, whether they like it or not."

"Good for you!" Bruce Hayes called out. "I didn't think that in the consumer field you had that kind of spirit! I didn't really mean that, Colin, but there's a point I overlooked. As most people know, salesmen selling insurance always try to obtain leads from their clients. In fact we teach trainees that that is one of the most important aspects of their work and they must never leave a client without asking him for referrals. I should imagine something similar might apply to many businesses. 'Use your users to get more users' is a good direct mail slogan. Don't you agree, Mike?"

"Very much so!" said Harley. He paused only to glance at his notes, then went on, "I think we've covered most of the ground, but I would like to conclude by riding my own hobby-horse. Direct mailing is a money spinner for retailers both large and small; it gives a smaller business an edge even against the giants. In my present world of books, the booksellers are not helped very much by publishers but, on the other hand, they don't help themselves either. How many booksellers list their customers? How many segment their lists so that they know which customer likes what – archaeology, history, romance, sport . . .? If they did, they could then mail these customers when new books arrive from the publishers, or even before they arrive. The customers would be delighted and would look upon it as a special service. It would pay handsome dividends."

Cathy asked, "May I have a final word?"

"You always do!" said Harley, laughing with the others.

Cathy pretended to be angry, then smiled and said, "It's amazing that people do buy from direct mail without seeking competitive prices. It probably isn't so strange to those in the speciality field. In our direct selling activities we know that speciality salesmen can call on shopkeepers, hotel managers, factory managers . . . and interest them immediately in appliances, products and services ranging from a few up to thousands of pounds. In many cases we get an order on the first call from buyers who would normally always seek competitive quotations. But only those who sell direct know the truth of this statement and no one can really give the reason, except that decisions are made quickly because of the salesman's skills and persuasiveness – and, of course, ability to add up all those benefits so that the buyer feels there is no need to hesitate.

"Surely the same applies to direct mailing, especially when free trials are offered? Orders are sent without thought of seeking other quotations, which is another good reason for launching more direct mail campaigns."

Harley said, "Thank you, Cathy. Now, are there any final contributions?"

Receiving no response he continued, "It's been a good week. I'm sure that when we say goodbye tomorrow we shall all feel that we have enjoyed ourselves and learned a great deal from each other."

The team applauded its agreement to Harley's closing words.

19 Sales Training

The team was in an end-of-term mood on Thursday evening. Drake and Ashton had completed their contributions, while Bruce Hayes and Cathy James were eagerly looking forward to talking on their favourite subject – sales training.

From their dinner table came loud laughter and the continual clinking of glasses. Other hotel guests quickly caught the mood; there was an interchange of banter. Then suddenly everyone was clinking glasses and, to the joy of the management, ordering more wine. The party spirit climaxed with an impromptu dance when everyone including the hotel owners joined in. Harley had not taken part in the celebrations. His meetings in London did not finish until 2 a.m. and left him no alternative but to stay in town.

He drove to Pellew next morning, arriving with only minutes to spare before the first session. Cathy awaited him in the drive. She no longer objected to a very warm hug and kiss and a whirl in the air which did her headache no good, followed by an even more loving hug and kiss. As they hurried to the hotel entrance hand-in-hand Harley said, "It's all OK, Cathy. The dinner party is on tonight." And that was all. A few moments later Harley entered the conference room, looking fresh and alert. "All's well?" he asked. There was a concerted groan of "No."

"Right, let's make a start and later we'll celebrate with a champagne lunch."

"Oh no," was again chorused.

Harley grinned. "As bad as that, was it?"

"Worse," said Ashton. "At my age I should have known better."

"But it was fun," added Drake. They agreed on that, then Harley said, "The final session and the last chapter in the book is on sales training. Our two experts will now take over. First Bruce on induction training, then Cathy on training in the field. Any questions?"

"Yes," said Drake, "Are you covering the qualities of an instructor?"

"No," replied Hayes. "They vary so much, but only a dedicated enthusiast will turn trainees into professional salesmen."

Ashton asked, "Are you covering visual aids and the use of computers etc.?"

"Again, no," said Hayes. "There can't be anyone involved in sales training who is not aware of the need to use all modern teaching aids. In my opinion the success of a training course depends solely on the skill of the instructors, but in the hands of a competent instructor the imaginative use of visual aids will undoubtedly increase his effectiveness."

Harley asked, "Any other questions?" There were none.

So he continued. "It may be thought that induction sales training applies more to the sales manager than the marketing director. That is wrong. Unfortunately many sales managers and sales training managers do not give sufficient thought to the building of a highly effective course; one which will send the trainee away with all the information needed to cover every eventuality, but also with improved selling skills and the confidence to try just that bit harder. Who, then, should check on the excellence of the course? Surely, the marketing director?

If he is fully aware of the ground to be covered he will be able to insist on the course being outstanding in every way.

"If the sales manager is also the marketing manager then he must check on himself. Too often induction training consists of a walk around the factory, discussions with various managers and a week or so in the field with an area manager. This is not adequate training. Selling is a matter of confidence. Marketing people are apt to believe that because a salesman has a good record he can sell any product or service without difficulty. This is not so. Without attending a proper induction course even very good salesmen may make an indifferent start. It is so difficult to make non-salesmen understand what lack of confidence means. Field sales managers rarely teach basics; they haven't the time. They expect the salesman to do as they do, which may not suit the character of the salesman at all.

"The usual excuse for not running an induction course is 'I only engage one salesman at a time, or two at the most'. This is no excuse. That one person should still go through a full induction course. It is time well spent for a sales manager, especially those whose turnover of salesmen is high or who are not satisfied with the results achieved by their salesmen.

"Finally, however experienced a salesman may be he will have formed bad habits and forgotten valuable basic principles. All salesmen, experienced or not, should attend an induction course followed by field training.

"Now over to you Bruce."

Hayes began. "The questions the training manager must ask himself are:

What *must* the trainee know?
What *should* the trainee know?
What *would it be nice* for the trainee to know?

"All *musts* will be included and as many *shoulds* as time allows. What it is nice for them to know is the usual extraneous matter: anecdotes, some of which could be irrelevant, apocryphal stories relating to the early days of the company.

"There might be other needs: long-term negotiating, merchandising, finance, knowledge of budgeting . . .

"Assuming there are twelve aspects of selling which must be covered during the course, the instructor will write down each of the headings on a separate sheet of paper. Each will then be researched, using:

personal knowledge
information acquired from associates – sales executives, salesmen
information obtained from other personnel involved in marketing
administrative details as far as they apply to the salesmen.

"These are the four main objectives of a sales training indoctrination course. Other objectives may have to be added, depending upon the product/service being marketed.

"A course could last a week or three months according to the products, but because the majority of companies give a one-week product/sales training course we shall use this period of time as a case study.

"The course will commence at 9 a.m. on a Monday morning and each session will be of not more than forty-five minutes' duration. As the human brain can only assimilate a reasonable amount of information at one time and salesmen tire quickly while listening, the breaks will be frequent and the course will finish at 5 p.m. each day. Here is a typical first day which applies to most companies.

"Session 1 is an introduction. During this session confidence will be established by the instructor detailing the company history and his own background. He will emphasise the opportunities with the company and the assistance given by back-up teams. He will cover briefly the marketing policy, plans for growth and the importance of the salesman in the marketing plan.

"The main objective during this session is for the instructor to win over the trainees, to arouse their enthusiasm, to alleviate their nervousness and to begin the long job of ensuring that the sales force will have pride in the company and in the work they do. Also of greatest importance, he must win the confidence of the trainees in himself, as an instructor.

"Session 2 covers the 'right mental attitude'. The instructor will explain in detail its meaning: the salesman's attitude towards head office, to the service department, to his customers and to his daily work. The objective of the instructor is to influence the mind of the trainees; to implant a long-lasting lesson of positive thinking. This also means inspiring the trainee to *want* to learn at the course and then work and sell in the right way.

"Setting objectives is a standard practice in all forms of training, but every instructor must remember that setting an objective does not mean that either a trainee or an experienced salesman will keep to that objective. For example, a target of eight calls a day might be an objective, but unless salesmen are persuaded or inspired to make those eight calls the instructor's objective will not be reached.

"The instructor, as well as the trainee, must have the 'right mental attitude'.

"Session 3 is on product information. The extent to which this is included will depend on the complexity of the product and the extent of the range. It would be unrealistic for the distributor of building materials to attempt to cover 8,000 products on offer and the knowledge of the detailed formulation of a chemical product may not always be essential, nor desirable. What the trainee wants, and this must always be the criterion, is all the information which will help him to sell. By far the best method of implanting product information is product analysis, to show the features and performance as benefits and buying reasons.

"This is of real practical value, and is explained in Session 6. However, some basic information about the product range should be given during this early session.

"For highly technical products there might have to be a separate training course, or several sessions in the sales training course.

"Session 4 is about sales presentation. During this session the instructor explains the advantages of a salesman working to a logical sales sequence, so that nothing is left to chance.

"The instructor will have to be persevering, enthusiastic and determined if he is to persuade some of the more experienced salesmen present of the benefits of a sales presentation. This is a challenge to the instructor and one that he must win if he is to ensure the success of the course.

"His objective is to obtain agreement, step by step, that a logical presentation is the only certain way of ensuring that an order will not be lost through any misunderstanding, on the part of the buyer, of the total sales offer.

"Session 5 is on motivating the buyer. The instructor will explain that there is usually a main motive and subsidiary motives behind every human action and a motive which influences one person may not apply to another, although both may have similar objectives.

"These facets of human behaviour, accepted by most anthropologists, psychologists and scientists, have a direct application to decision-makers.

1. Buyers, while usually having a main buying motive, are also swayed by subsidiary motives.
2. Buyers employed by different companies may buy the same product from the same supplier but for different reasons.

"One salesman may have a price advantage, another an efficiency advantage, a third a design or promotion advantage over competitors, but each may lose orders by thinking only in terms of motivating a buyer because of the one potential advantage. While a buyer might appear to be mainly interested in design, he could also be motivated by security. The salesman who drives home the price advantage may not realise that the profit from repeat business, which the customer is obtaining because of the ready demand for a competitor's product, motivates the buyer more than an immediate gain.

"Each of these salesmen may well be able to cope with the buyer's fears, or need for security or increased profitability through repeat business, but overlook the need for dealing with these motives.

"A trainee might ask: 'But if people are motivated to act in different ways to reach a similar objective, how can I know which main motivator to use in my sales offer? Also, how do I discover subsidiary motivators?'

"Regular calling will enable him to learn the motivators applying to individual buyers. He will also learn by observation, by asking the buyer questions and by listening to and assessing his replies. But the instructor will point out that every salesman should include in his sales offer all the prime and subsidiary motivators applicable to his merchandise, product or service. If a product or service has a different application for different buyers, it is perfectly feasible to use selective motivators.

"The instructor will emphasise that the salesman's objective must always be to try to include in his sales offer the motivational force or forces which will impel the buyer to buy.

"Session 6 is the sales offer analysis. A salesman must be able to prove to himself that he is selling the right product and offer analysis provides that proof, enabling him to identify all product features and derive from them every single buyer benefit. It is the accumulation of these benefits which gives proof of the value of the product.

"Session 7 continues with a sales offer analysis exercise. While, in Session 6, the instructor explains the meaning of offer analysis and the fact that analysis involves thinking in depth, in this session the instructor, in conjunction with the trainees, will build up the total offer of his product or service.

"Session 8 is a summary and question time. The instructor will summarise briefly the day's work and then invite questions. These will apply to all the sessions, in spite of the fact that during each session the trainees will have had the opportunity both of asking and answering questions."

Hayes invited questions.

Cathy said, "In our practical offer analysis sessions we provide offer analysis forms to be completed by the trainees. There are three columns on the form, the first is for product features, the second for benefits derived from the features and the third column translates the benefits into buyer appeal. Mike, I can let you have a form if you want to use it in the book."

Harley shook his head. "It would take up space for no purpose. The explanation is clear enough, but thank you, Cathy – and it's back to you, Bruce."

Hayes said, "I won't detail the following day's work, only the ground to be covered:

1. Regular re-caps: summaries and checks.
2. Teaching the three main steps in the presentation: opening, selling benefits and close.

The objective is to show trainees how to obtain the undivided attention of the buyer and to ensure that they do not, by a bad approach, antagonise, annoy or bore him, or in any way lose his attention. It gives the trainee an advantage over many salesmen who believe that an approach is an opportunity for a chat.

The main body of the presentation is derived from offer analysis, all buyer 'benefits' being given in a logical sequence.

The close is a key session. If a salesman has fundamental character weaknesses he will only obtain the easy order and will eventually fail, or fall into the rut of mediocrity. Most salesmen, however, are weak on closing orders, often because of some inherent fear of upsetting the buyer.

High pressure is never needed to close sales; it only antagonises buyers. All that is required is to 'nudge' the buyer into agreeing to place an order or arrive at a decision. If more than a nudge is needed, the sales offer has failed.

The instructor will explain to the trainees the various closing techniques.

3. Although the course is still in its early stages, the sooner the trainees practise a sales presentation the better. There are three main techniques used for involving the trainees in a 'mock' selling situation:

(a) The instructor with a colleague enacts the part of salesman and buyer. The delegates watch and later criticise. On the face of it this should be good teaching, but there is a risk of the instructor and his colleague developing into actors, becoming too good to be true. The nervous salesman may then feel that he is facing a very difficult task, far beyond his capabilities.

(b) The trainees take turns in enacting the parts of buyer and salesman. The other trainees watch and criticise or make positive suggestions for improvement. This, however, has disadvantages. Salesmen are not actors.

(c) The trainees form syndicates of three. One is the buyer, one the salesman and a third the adjudicator. The adjudicator can stop the sale at any time to pinpoint a mistake or to offer advice. This is usually the best form of sales demonstration.

(d) Videos of demonstration – after some proficiency has been acquired.

4. There must be a session on competitor analysis. The instructor will conduct this session on strictly factual lines. It is a mistake for the instructor to brush aside the competitors' strengths and over-emphasise their weakness. The claim, 'We are the finest', 'We are the greatest', 'We are the best', does not help the salesmen when facing buyers.
5. Obviously there will be a session on answering objections. The instructor's objective is to make sure that the salesman can answer all possible objections and answer them correctly. Research will have provided a list of the standard objections used by prospects/customers.
6. There should be one or two sessions on obtaining interviews. The session will be adapted to line up with the product/service being sold. The objective is to show the salesmen how they can contact the decision maker, whether he be the managing director, departmental head, personnel manager or any other executive. The various techniques for obtaining appointments will be covered: telephoning, letter-writing, cold calling, advising clients in advance of visits etc.
7. Other sessions will cover territory planning and problem solving. The instructor will explain that everything marketed should help to solve a problem: meeting a demand for consumer goods, helping to increase production, improving efficiency, providing

added security, comfort etc. This session will highlight customer problems and how the unit/service/merchandise can help to overcome them.

8. Other sessions will cover any of the following subjects, depending on the type of product/service:
   administration
   public relations
   advertising
   demonstrating
   merchandising
   handling difficult buyers
   product mix
   lectures by other managers: services, works.
9. The final session will be solely inspirational covering, perhaps, human relations.
10. Each sales trainer will have to adapt this prototype five-day course to suit his own marketing policy, but it will be found that very few of these sessions can be omitted. There should be a great deal of trainee participation, syndicates etc.

"And that," said Hayes, "concludes my main contribution to the book."

Everyone applauded the excellent summary of an induction course.

After a coffee break Harley said, "Cathy, you were a highly successful field trainer, so tell us your recipe for successful sales training."

Cathy began. "It's an honour to be allowed to give the final session of our marketing week. First I'll list the objectives of the field trainer.

1. Agree sensible targets and ensure that these targets are reached.

2. Motivate salesmen to keep to company policies: terms, deliveries, prices etc.
3. Set the objectives for the team and ensure that they are met.
4. Inaugurate and carry out an appraisal programme so that each member of the team knows his own strengths and weaknesses and what he has to do to achieve promotion.
5. Create complete co-operation between salesmen and branch office or head office or service division.
6. Provide head office with carefully considered forecasts.
7. Hold and control regular sales meetings.
8. Ensure that company property is maintained: car, sales aids, samples.
9. Give objective reports on customers'/prospects' credit standing.
10. Organise selling efforts to match demands from head office.
11. Ensure customer goodwill.
12. Be without prejudice in all circumstances.
13. Be loyal under all circumstances or leave the company.
14. Provide head office with accurate reports on salesmen, territory, customers.
15. Show salesmen how to sell a complete range.
16. Carry out a sales audit to assess share of market and potential growth.
17. Regularly help head office in updating salesmen's job specification.
18. Insist on essential paper work only; demands from head office are often irrational.
19. Assist in the full sales training programme.
20. Advise on the improvement of sales aids.
21. Advise how to interview and select potential star salesmen.

22. Enable salesmen of limited ability to reach the limit of their capacity, thus realising their potential.

"The field sales manager should prove to his salesmen that their interests are his interests and that they have a common objective. They must be convinced that his demands on them are for their benefit as well as for the collective good of the company as a whole.

"Before working with a salesman a good field sales manager will always do his homework. He will study the previous one, two or three months' reports, according to when he last worked with the particular salesman. He will refer to his own reports, so that he will know the salesman's problems at work and, possibly, at home.

"From his homework he will discover:

(a) what lesson he had emphasised at the previous meeting, and whether or not it had been applied by the salesman. If not, why not?
(b) a list of problem customers
(c) a list of queries which have been raised by the salesman relating to commission, service, delivery, pricing etc.
(d) the area in which they should concentrate their efforts
(e) the main new lesson he will cover during his visit. It could be: how to obtain more interviews, how to open new accounts, how to sell benefits, how to use sales aids more efficiently, revision of product knowledge, the manner in which the salesman keeps his records, methods of working territory etc.

"Now on to working with my superb sales girls, oh sorry, I mean salesmen.

"In advance of each call a decision has to be made as to who will control the interviews. Buyers do not like 'twin attacks', but they do not object to a dual interview if only one of the representatives gives the presentation and mostly answers his questions.

"With a fairly new salesman the field sales manager will control all the interviews on the first day. On the second day the salesman will control each interview, with no interference from the field sales manager.

"With well established salesmen the plan will vary and most of the selling will be carried out by the salesman. Subsequently the field sales manager will either be generous in his praise or he will explain the ways in which the salesman can improve his selling skills.

"Salesmen can be like children – petulant, difficult, argumentative, obstinate, unreasonable . . . But they will not be won over or have their attitudes changed by a field sales manager who is also difficult, argumentative, obstinate, or even petulant.

"This is the way to coach salesmen:

(a) inspire them – arouse their enthusiasm so that they will want to learn
(b) never coach them in front of a buyer
(c) after each interview there should be a kerb/car conference, during which the field sales manager will analyse the sales presentation first by inviting the salesman's views and then adding his own comments
(d) never sap a salesman's confidence by insisting on his using a selling technique or skill which at that stage of his career he feels incapable of carrying out – if he makes mistakes on his own he will soon recover, in front of a manager he will feel unhappy for a very long time and he will sell badly if his confidence has been shaken
(e) at the end of the day, review the whole day's work."

Cathy then invited questions.

Ashton said, "Didn't you find it both tiring and boring to work for two or three days with someone you had nothing in common with?"

"But we did have a big issue in common – getting orders."

"Yes, but you had lunch to get through and the

evenings for listening to their moans and stories about their love lives or whatever."

"Ian, you are a brilliant marketing manager but you've never been a field trainer, have you?"

Ashton shook his head in agreement.

Cathy said, "If you had you would find that 90 per cent of those you work with are enthusiasts, they want to talk selling all the time. The other 10 per cent may need personal advice and a good field manager must act many parts: a psychologist, lawyer, accountant, part diplomat, an ambassador and a leader, but most of all a motivator."

Ashton smiled and said, "I wouldn't have made a very good field manager."

"You would if you had been with our group. Field managers need training every bit as much as salesmen. Mostly a sales manager will pick on one of his best salesmen to take over an area. But stars are not always good teachers. They expect trainees to be able to copy their own style of selling which might not be possible for a newcomer. The answer is to train field managers in training. We do and we've never had a real failure. Satisfied, Ian?"

Ashton asked, "Is it too late for me to work for you?"

After the laughter died down Cathy continued. "Now for a real headache, handling problem salesmen. Problem salesmen can generally be classified as those in a comfortable rut; those who take it easy; the unhappy and depressed and those who become prima donnas or over-ambitious.

"Both average and top-class salesmen can settle into ruts. They believe that they can only continue to increase sales if provided with new products, better advertising, different sales aids, a part-time assistant . . .

"The field sales manager can show by example what can be achieved by extra effort and a changed mental attitude. He could offer increased commission over and above the sales limit being achieved, or try to discover what incentive would motivate the salesman to try harder.

"Investigate all the areas in which the salesman could increase sales: improved method of working his territory, to enable him to make more calls; trying harder to open new accounts; giving even better assistance to his customers so that more repeat business may be obtained.

"Consider the salesman who takes things easy. Perhaps he is not in a rut, but is apt to 'ease off' on occasion. The cause could be boredom with his work or too many outside interests, often resulting in his becoming so immersed in these activities that time is taken off from selling in order to attend meetings etc.

"The field sales manager must find out the real reason why the salesman is taking things easy. Perhaps he has problems at home which take priority over his work.

"We now move on to the depressed salesman. The field sales manager must discover the true reason for this unhappiness. He must be like the sages of old, listening patiently and neither agreeing nor disagreeing, his objective being to provide another solution to a difficult problem. In the first place the salesman will prevaricate, but when he knows that the field sales manager is reliable and trustworthy he may tell the whole story.

"And now we come to the prima donna – but nearly all star salesmen are prima donnas at some time or another. Their intransigence, obstinacy and demands are all part of their star quality and are of little consequence. Usually they are most reasonable people at heart and a flare-up one day will be forgotten the next. Sometimes, however, their demands cannot be met and this can lead to their sulking; or they can become obstinate and, for example, refuse to send in reports on a regular basis.

"To handle the prima donna when he is in one of his moods the field sales manager must be careful never to make him feel unimportant – in fact, the reverse – but when he makes one of his unreasonable demands, it must be made clear to him that although the sales director and everyone at head office think the world of him and appreciate everything he does, on this one occasion he has to fall in line because . . .

"The field sales manager must show that although he is kindly, he can also be tough.

"Finally, there is the over-ambitious salesman. Every field manager will at some time have one of these in his team, whose ambition is far ahead of his abilities.

"At regular intervals he will let it be known that he is disappointed at not being recognised for his true worth by the company's executives. He will continually hint at other jobs which he has only refused out of loyalty to the company, but that loyalty should not be strained too far. Unfortunately so many over-ambitious people do not have the qualifications nor the qualities to match their ambitions.

"The field sales manager must do his best to retain such men, but he faces not only a man problem; there is usually a wife problem as well. Deep down the wife may well know that her husband is not as brilliant as he believes himself to be, but for all that she will force herself to think she is married to a selling genius who is not appreciated. Also, of course, she wants the extra money that would go with the better job.

"Usually the over-ambitious salesman does not have the courage to leave and try to get a better job. What he needs is a sop to his ambition. If it is possible give such a man additional work of which he is capable, for example assisting a new salesman when the field sales manager is not available, or a title which shows that the company appreciate his worth. This is often sufficient to keep him happy for a time. He will, however, need continual guidance and a lot of patience from his field sales manager.

"That's all about problem salesmen," said Cathy. "Now on to time planning.

"The most important point to remember when we are time planning is that ninety-nine people out of a hundred, a guess maybe, never have the time to do what they don't want to do.

"Here are some objectives for the field sales manager:

1. Check on wasted time: travelling, morning coffee, discussing extraneous matters.
2. Check on overhead times: signing mail, reading reports, attending meetings. Can they be cut down?
3. Most time is lost through lack of proper organisation. List each day the six tasks which must be accomplished that day and ensure that they are completed.
4. Delegate whenever possible, but not the tasks that you are fearful of tackling – for example, calling on a problem customer.
5. Break down all large assignments into steps and set time targets for the completion of each step.

"It is a cliché, but worth repeating, that thirty minutes a day wasted is two-and-a-half hours a week, ten hours a month or, excluding holidays, possibly eighty or ninety hours a year, approximately eleven working days. But the average time wasted is nearer to one hour a day, approximately twenty-two working days a year, and this applies both to salesmen and to field sales managers.

"Now let us look at the ways that some field managers fritter away their time.

1. They do not make the first call with the salesman at an early time when a buyer could be available for the interview. There is nothing sacrosanct about 9 a.m. when buyers are on duty at 8 a.m.
2. There should never be a morning coffee break during working time. The break for coffee between ten-thirty and eleven, the best time of the day for obtaining interviews, is quite wrong.

3. Field sales managers spend too much time with their best salesmen. Being only human they can hardly be blamed; it is enjoyable working with an outstanding salesman. The rule should be: spend less time with the star salesman, he should be able to look after himself. Spend longer with the average salesman to try to turn him into a star.
4. The field sales manager should plan his work with the objective of saving travelling time. He should ask himself these questions:

   How often is it necessary to work with each man?
   How long should I spend with each man?
   Is it possible to work with two salesmen on adjacent territories for shorter periods, rather than with one salesman for a long period, necessitating long journeys in two successive weeks?
5. The field sales manager should think constantly of how to increase the effective call ratio of his salesmen.
6. Should territories be adjusted or cut to save the time of salesmen and field sales managers?
7. The duration of telephone calls to head offices should be cut.
8. Train salesmen in time saving. On every visit the field sales manager should refer to the value of saving time. Salesmen quickly form bad time-wasting habits. They start work late and finish too early; take off the odd afternoon; spend time at home telephoning, using this as an excuse to do some gardening or help the wife arrange a party and, especially, they will waste time by bad planning of their work.

"A very good basis for a meeting of salesmen is to pose the questions: How can we save more time? How can we stop wasting time?

"And that's all," said Cathy.

Everyone applauded and Ian, Bruce and Colin took the opportunity of showing their admiration by kissing her.

Cathy thanked them demurely and said, "All I did was give some extracts from our own course for field sales managers. I must have sounded like an instructor, rather than someone giving an informal talk."

Harley said, "You got it just right, Cathy, but all our contributions will be edited." Then standing up he added, "You don't want a long closing speech, but I must say how much in your debt I am, not only for your contributions and co-operation but for your constant cheerfulness and friendship, which I know will continue."

There were more kisses for Cathy, much handshaking and back slapping, and then Harley said, "Now on to our champagne lunch and we'll all meet again for a party when *Marketing Strategy in Action* is published."

Before hurrying off for his drive back to London, Harley reminded Cathy that she was to meet him in the lobby of the Hyatt Carlton Tower Hotel that evening at seven-thirty.

20 The Harley Strategy

To Harley, punctuality meant being fifteen minutes early for an appointment. At 7.10 he was in the lobby of the Hyatt Carlton Tower Hotel, infuriated because others who believed that a 7.30 p.m. appointment meant arriving at 7.30 had not yet shown up. At 7.25 Cathy arrived, looking glamorous in a figure-hugging pale blue silk dress.

"You're late!" was his friendly greeting.

Ignoring the remark Cathy said, "First you try to bed me with the corniest of routines, then you propose marriage with the affection a dog shows for a cat. You delight in telling me all your bad news, but refuse to explain your reasons for optimism. This morning you gave me peremptory instructions to be here at 7.30 sharp, when everything would be explained. I can't understand why I, Cathy James, so used to giving orders and controlling others, should meekly accept your instructions."

Harley took her by the arm. "Only because you love me," he said.

A few minutes later, on the first floor, they were greeted by the restaurant manager of the Chelsea Room. "I have your table ready, Mr Harley, and I've also reserved a table in the lounge for you. Chef asked me to tell him when you arrived, so that he can begin preparing your meal." He led the way to the lounge and fussed round Cathy, making sure she was comfortably seated. A waiter came over:

"Would you like the champagne served now, Mr Harley?"

"No, we'll wait for our guests to arrive."

Harley spent the next five minutes trying to pacify Cathy. Then walking towards them came a middle-aged man with dark hair accompanied by a plumpish lady wearing rather a fixed smile. Harley jumped to his feet and warmly greeted his guests.

Following introductions, he beckoned the waiter, who expertly extracted the champagne cork and filled the glasses.

Harley said, "This is an evening for celebration and I hope you will agree with the actions I have taken on your behalf. The Chelsea Room chef is one of the greats and I've asked him to prepare a meal suitable for the occasion. I know you are both gourmets and enjoy nothing better than a gourmet's holiday." Turning to Cathy he added, "Molly has written a cookbook and a wine book and she regularly assists Turner & Deeping, the wine merchants, to select their wines."

"Wonderful!" said Cathy, who had badly misjudged Molly, thinking her a suburban housewife more used to attending women's guild meetings.

Harley said, "Cathy is an old friend of mine and knows what has happened, although not the final outcome."

Cathy turned to Molly. "All men are the same, aren't they?" she said. "Little boys at heart, enjoying their secret societies."

Molly agreed and they all laughed and toasted each other.

Harley said, "Well, this is the full story." He looked at his watch. "Assuming that we shall be here until eight-fifteen, I'll arrange for dinner to be served at eight-thirty."

The restaurant manager hovering in the background

came across as Harley nodded towards him, accepted the news and departed to relay it to the chef. Cathy said, "I don't know why you don't use a stopwatch, Mike."

"That's a good idea! I'll get one." Mike relaxed in his chair amidst more laughter and said, "I'll begin at the end. With the full blessing of his wife, and that means a lot, Reg Panton is joining Harley's."

Cathy said, "That much I guessed, when you introduced us. How did it happen?"

"Be patient! I'll tell you my part of the story and then Reg will tell you his," he continued. "By sheer coincidence I met Reg at the Garrick, soon after my meeting with Corbett."

Cathy thought, 'I doubt whether there was any coincidence at all, knowing Mike'.

She heard Harley saying, "Reg told me no secrets, but he was obviously not happy at Corbett's takeover of Brooke & Dean, nor with Corbett's management by dictate. No one at Brooke & Dean felt that their job was safe. We met again a few weeks later and he seemed even less happy. Now you go on with the story, Reg."

Panton said, "After Mike's meeting with Joe Corbett, Joe made it clear to me that he intended to close down Harley's. I didn't like that attitude. Dynamic, no doubt, but completely alien to the publishing world in which I have spent so many years.

"I had to give instructions to the Browser bookshop buyers, without giving them any adequate reasons, to purchase as little as possible from Harley's. Very secretly I had to contact Kenneth Jason, again much against my principles, and persuade him to leave Harley's and join us at Brooke & Dean.

"I didn't take any action for some time. I delayed as long as possible, until Corbett called me in one day and said that either I did his bidding – those were his exact words – or I could get out. So much against the grain I did his bidding, and you know the rest.

"Jason, Chapman and a couple of salesmen are joining Brooke & Dean and so are two of your best authors, Lilian Greystone and Hugo Parkins.

"When I was feeling at my lowest at the beginning of this week Mike approached me. He asked me how I felt about having Jason as joint managing director, how my editorial staff felt about working with Susan Clifford and how our sales manager felt about being upgraded to marketing manager which, he knew, meant very little. He and Chapman would have to work together on the same terms, irrespective of titles.

"Corbett's great weakness is that he doesn't understand people, how they think, how they react. He believes that if they are paid enough he can get anyone to do anything. But that only happens if there are no alternatives and you, Mike, came along with an alternative. You offered us all jobs, you did a Corbett in reverse and, Mike, you were most persuasive."

"I'm sure of that!" said Cathy. "I know him."

"I'm glad he was," said Panton. "Everyone in the publishing world has always thought most highly of the Harley Brothers. We at Brooke & Dean used to be like Harley's, until Corbett took us over. I made my decision yesterday and so did the others. Now you carry on, Mike."

Cathy couldn't help admiring Harley for the way he had taken on Corbett and beaten him.

Harley continued. "When Reg told me that the others were willing to leave, I offered positions to their sales manager, Richard White, who will become our sales manager, and to their editorial director, Peggy Wiseman. I didn't confirm the offer to Peggy until I had spoken to Susan and put her in the picture. If she had said no, Peggy would have had to stay at Corbett's, but Susan was delighted. She wants to build up a list of romantic fiction, while Peggy is keen to develop our books in the technical field. That will be an ideal combination."

Then turning to Panton he said, "Now tell us what happened when you saw Corbett this morning."

Panton smiled grimly. "I told him why I and the others were leaving him. We would all give the statutory notice. His answer was, 'You won't! You'll get out now, and the others! I'll sue Harley for enticement.' I thought that was really rich, but I believe he meant it. Tycoons like Corbett never can see any point of view other than their own.

"So we shall all be joining Harley's. I don't want to do a Corbett, but I have the feeling that some of our authors with whom I have been in close contact for many years will eventually join Harley's list too. I know this trade just as well as Jason, if not better, and Richard White is a first-class sales manager. Chapman isn't even in his league! You told me the truth about Harley's position at the moment, Mike, but that doesn't matter. It's the future that counts and it's going to be a great future. I've been given a new lease of life and I'll do my best."

They all drank to the success of Harley's, as the restaurant manager arrived to say that the first course, *foie gras frais au cerfeuil*, was ready.

It was 11 p.m. when Harley and Cathy said 'goodbye' to the Pantons, after much kissing and hand-shaking.

Harley took Cathy's arm. "We've won a great victory!"

"You're marvellous!" said Cathy. "You really are."

"Do you mean that?"

"Of course I do." He turned and kissed her.

"You've had too much to drink, Mike, to drive home," she said. "You'd better take a taxi."

"No, thanks."

"I think you should!"

"Why? We're staying here."

"We're what?"

"We're staying here. I booked accommodation."

"One double bedroom, I presume?"

"Now, would I do a thing like that?"

"Yes!"

"Well I haven't! I've booked two double rooms, but . . ."

"But what?"

"They do have communicating doors."

"You never give up, Mike, do you?"

"Never!"

MARKETING STRATEGY IN ACTION

Also by Alfred Tack

MARKETING AND MANAGEMENT BOOKS

Executive Development
Building, Training, and Motivating a Sales Force
How to Overcome Nervous Tension and Speak Well in Public
How to Double Your Income in Selling
1000 Ways to Increase your Sales
Sell Better – Live Better
Sell Your Way to Success
How to Train Yourself to Succeed in Selling
How to Increase Sales by Telephone
Profitable Letter Writing
How to Increase Your Sales to Industry
How to Succeed in Selling
How to Sell Successfully Overseas
Professional Salesmanship
Successful Sales Management
Marketing, The Sales Manager's Role
How to Succeed as a Sales Manager
Motivational Leadership
The High Quality Manager

FICTION

The Great Hijack
The Spy Who wasn't Exchanged
The Top Steal
Forecast–Murder
Murder Takes Over
P A to Murder
Death Kicks a Pebble
Selling's Murder
Interviewing's Killing
The Prospect's Dead
The Test Match Murder
A Murder is Staged
Killing Business
Death Takes a Dive
Return of the Assassin